ALWAYS THE FIRST

(Risk-Taking. Sassy. Victorious)

By

LYNN HAWKINS, PH.D

The Story of Annie Mae Walker:
Survival in an Uncivil World

ISBN: 978-1-943789-34-4
Copyright 2016

This book may be purchased through
    Amazon.com and Amazon Kindle,
    Taylor and Seale Publishing
    www.taylorandsealeeducation.com.
    Barnes and Noble
    Books a Million

Taylor and Seale Publishing, LLC.
Daytona Beach, Florida 32118
Phone: 1-888-866-8248
www.taylorandseale.com

Dedication

To Dr. Evan Rivers,

Whose inspiration and compassion made it
possible for me to achieve my dreams.

Preface

"I was always the first," Mae Walker recalls: either the first woman or the first Black or the first Black woman,"

At age 6 she became the first Black girl to attend kindergarten in Florida, then the first scholar mentored by Mary McLeod Bethune, Zora Neale Hurston, and Eleanor Roosevelt, the first valedictorian of the first four-year Black high school at Bethune-Cookman and the first summa cum laude graduate of the first four-year class of Bethune-Cookman College.

She was the first Black teacher to petition the Florida legislature for equal pay, the first woman Civil Rights leader targeted and bombed by the Ku Klux Klan in two states, hers the first home Malcolm X lived in while waiting for a mosque, and the first Black university professor in the North to serve as a captain for Dr. Martin Luther King, Jr., joining civil rights marches at Selma, Alabama, and Washington, D.C.

She was the first Black to receive a Master's Degree at Bank Street College and the first Black to get a teaching position in the all-white private school in New York. She was the first M.A. in sociology at Adelphi University, the first Black woman professor and first Black Ph.D. at the State University of New York-Stony Brook.

The first Black on the Human Rights Commission, Dr. Walker was the founder of the first Head Start program in New York, the creator of the first African-American

Studies program at a New York University, the first Black woman Danforth Scholar at Yale University, and the first and only half-Seminole/half Black anthropologist in the world. She became the first long-time survivor of sarcoma, cancer of the spine, living 19 years after being told she had six months left. "The doctors say I'm a living miracle."

"Being the first at everything wasn't hard at all," Dr. Walker said, "because I decided a long time ago that in almost every situation where a Black enters, you have to be considered outstanding to even get in. With that, I was always given, not patronage, but great respect for the contribution I was making."

That was not true, of course, for white supremacists in both Florida and New York, she said. "They kept trying to murder me."

Table of Contents

Chapters

Introduction

Mae Walker's life shows how "one wise child" can grow up to change America for its citizens of color—with a little help from her friends: Eleanor Roosevelt, Jesse Jackson, Adam Clayton Powell, Maya Angelou, Mary McLeod Bethune, Malcolm X, Dr. Martin Luther King, Jr., Marilyn Monroe, Ella Fitzgerald, and Paule Marshall, among others. The impoverished black child from a Florida turpentine camp became the adult who created and pioneered the model for both Head Start and for Black Studies programs at the State University of New York, and garnered a Ph.D. in anthropology. The only half Seminole half Black anthropologist in the world, she traveled to Africa and researched the folkways of tribes in Nigeria, Ghana, the Ivory Coast, Liberia, Tanzania, Kenya and Uganda. In the U.S. Mae served as a leader in Civil Rights from the time of the first of several Ku Klux Klan attempts on her life.

It's hard to imagine her beginning life, how a situation could have been more hopeless. Born January 7, 1913, in a shanty at a Florida turpentine camp to an impoverished, black Gullah-speaking father and a Seminole mother who died when her daughter was three, Annie Mae McClary inherited a vicious stepmother who tried to decapitate her with a hatchet. And then life became worse.

Her seven brothers and sisters were split up and sent to different homes. She saw her adored father whipped by his white boss. There wasn't enough money for shoes, not even a nickel for the writing tablet Mae longed for. At an age when white children were in the first grade, she did the cooking at home and sewed her own and her little sister's clothes from old flour sacks.

In fact, the little girl was left with just one statement to live on: "You are one wise child who will be a teacher." Coming from an illiterate father in a Southern state which didn't even offer elementary education to black children, this belief would sound impossible — to an outsider. But by third grade, she was teaching basic literacy to her father and other men. Luckily for America, this granddaughter of slaves instead turned her father's promise into a reality not only for herself, but for millions of children under a program she pioneered: Head Start.

Along the way to both earned and honorary Ph.Ds., the indomitable Mae was mothered by Mary McLeod Bethune, who was considered the most influential black woman in America. At age six, Annie Mae became part of the first kindergarten class, then valedictorian of the first four-year high school class, and first summa cum laude graduate of Bethune-Cookman College's first baccalaureate program.

Mae sang for a United States President, whose wife, Eleanor Roosevelt, not only personally mentored the young black woman's education, but later brought her famous

Scottish terrier, Fala, to visit with Mae and her third-grade pupils at the Little Red Schoolhouse in New York.

On full scholarships to the Bank Street College of Education in New York City, then Adelphi University, she learned to speak thirteen languages. Dr. Walker was the first black woman Danforth Scholar at Yale University, where Maya Angelou and Paule Marshall sometimes stayed in her apartment. Malcolm X lived in her home, and she marched the streets of Selma, Alabama, and Washington D.C. with her good friend, Dr. Martin Luther King, Jr.

Mae also became the "best buddy" of writer Zora Neale Hurston and friends with Nobel prizewinner Toni Morrison; playwright Arthur Miller; actress Marilyn Monroe; and Eric Williams, the President of Trinidad. The love of her life, William Howard Walker, chauffeured the famous singer Ella Fitzgerald before Mae helped him to become a psychiatric social worker who helped disadvantaged children.

Mae escaped assassination attempts by the KKK, became friends with prime ministers, film stars, tycoons, and poets, and was initiated into the royalty of the Yoruba tribe. As a visiting professor in Ghana, in Dar es Salaam, Tanzania, and the West Indies, Mae became friends with prime ministers, film stars, tycoons, and poets. She wrote two texts on anthropology and a two-hour television special on the history of African-American churches before she retired from the State University of New York-Stony Brook in 1977.

After her "retirement" Mae began teaching at the college where she had grown up, Bethune-Cookman, then joined the faculty of Daytona Beach Community College (now Daytona State College) — taking her first actual piano lessons at seventy-four. At age eighty, she gave her first public performance of her favorite music, Beethoven's "Moonlight Sonata."

At eighty-four years old, this indomitable woman, the only known twenty-year survivor of osteosarcoma (cancer of the spine), Dr. Walker was still teaching college students at Daytona Beach Community College, which is where we accidentally discovered that a black Mae McClary Walker and white Lynn McClary Hawkins shared common ancestral roots all the way back to Ireland and Scotland. And that's how Mae began sharing her remarkable story with me.

This biography/autobiography is the result of more than 250 hours of audio-recorded interviews, as well as notes taken during classroom sessions with Dr. Walker telling stories to her students. The incidents related in this book were told as a series of anecdotal remembrances, some of them as we revisited the actual turpentine distillery and camp store, which have been reconstructed at the Barberville, Florida Pioneer Village. I compiled, arranged, and edited the stories, and Dr. Walker read the final texts. As well as interviews, I have included editor's notes on historical material which would amplify or document Dr. Walker's experiences when necessary to help readers understand the background of particular events or relationships with famous people in her life story.

As perhaps the only half Native American-half African-American anthropologist in the world, Mae Walker provides rare insight into the racist culture of her childhood on the reservation and in the tortuous existence of the Florida turpentine camp, into the emotionally-charged educational culture that she changed for America's black students, and the rich culture of the African nations she observed and shared. Her list of friends reads like an edition of *Who's Who*.

Because of her beliefs about the strong role of all women, Mae Walker addresses two fundamental goals of feminist research: 1) the rediscovery of lost role models, and 2) the reassessment of the roles and contributions of women in society, especially in the black communities in American and other parts of the world she has visited and lived.

One of her students announced, "Dr. Walker doesn't just teach Black History—she IS Black History." But more than a microcosm of the struggle of race, she is one of those keepers of the flame, showing through her life that one indomitable spirit can, indeed, change the world.

As the anthropologist wrote in her monograph, *Portraits of the John and Sarah Nunn Family Tree*:

> In the case of our use of the oral tradition, we have come to know that it is an invaluable source of reference when attempting to portray human images and evoke human emotions of identification with and empathy for the persons of whom we speak or write. Further, oral tradition has always been and still is a reliable source of history, used in most non-literate societies throughout the world. Besides, the term history itself means literally 'his' story, indicating the story as he/she understands it. Therefore, we believe that the oral history contained in this study is

sufficiently valid for the purpose of conveying at least some knowledge and gaining some understanding of our ancestral past.

The Black Women Oral History Project, a ten volume anthology, explains how the oral history interview, created by a questioner and a narrator, has become "a primary instrument for the collecting and telling of a people's history, breaking down myths and stereotypes as it fills gaps and corrects distortions and corruptions in the written documentary stories. It attempts to find out what is going on in the mind and heart. It asks, 'what did you feel and how do you feel' as it tries to explain the causes of actions. It focuses the picture. It says to someone, 'Tell me your story. Sing me your song.' This oral history deliberately creates primary source material for use by future historians."

The oral history is also the standard for biographies/ autobiographies of Native Americans—the maternal half of Dr. Walker's family tree. An anthropologist-researched biography, *Cobett Mack: the life of a Northern Paiute* by Michael Hittman quotes Arnold Krupat's comment that Indian biography is a contradiction in terms: Indian autobiographies are collaborative efforts jointly produced by some white person who translates, transcribes, compiles, edits, interprets, polishes and ultimately determines the 'form' of the text in writing, and by an Indian who is its 'subject' and whose life becomes the 'content' of the autobiography whose title may bear his name.

The word "his" is appropriate. "Until recently," researcher Caroline Steedman noted, "Women did not write autobiographies. Their lives were not deemed important enough to have biographies written about them."

As anthropologist Norman Denzen observes ,

Lives are arbitrary constructions, constrained by the cultural writing practices of the time. These cultural practices led to the inventions and influences of gendered, knowing others who can locate subjects within family social spaces where lives have beginnings, turning points, and clearly defined endings. Such texts create 'real' persons about whom truthful statements are presumably made. In fact, as argued above, these texts are narrative fictions, cut from the same kinds of cloth as the lives they tell about.

Denzen also states:

The autobiography, the root form of the biography, has been a central preoccupation of Western literature and the discourse of modernism at least since Augustine (AD 354-430) wrote in his *Confessions*, and has origins in the ancient civilizations of the Middle East

---

Editor's note: This material for this book was first published as a doctoral dissertation: *Wise Child, Wise Woman* by Dr. Lynn McClary Hawkins at the University of Nebraska-Lincoln in 1998, two months before Dr. Walker's death.

The Black Scholar 21 (4), 10-21. Examines Turner's work in Gullah, the Creole-English spoken exclusively by African-Americans along the coast of Georgia and South Carolina, and in the Sea Islands, and used in literature such as Joel Chandler Harris's *Uncle Remus: His Songs and His Sayings.* Notes features of Gullah include absence of final consonants and absence of *theta* and *eth.*

But the culture itself bequeathed a rare gift: "African customs and images were kept alive by nightly storytelling as 'liars' began to spin their yarns to two generations of Gullah children" (Smith 291). The liar was an itinerant, usually an older male who moved from one former plantation settlement to another, spinning animal tales (*Uncle Remus*, for example) and morality tales in exchange for food and shelter.

Death of a Childhood

I waked up in a world of hurt as Mrs. Lilla yanked my arm to pull me out of bed, switching red welts onto my arms and legs with the bare spirea branch.

"Annie Mae! I see them sheets. Now git out! A four year-old bed wetter is evil!" As she dragged me down barefooted on the rough pine floor, then out to the dirt yard, she shouted directions to her oldest daughter, who was fourteen. "Irene, go get an ax and a block of wood."

Then my new stepmother showed me the ax before she blindfolded my eyes with a rag. Pinching my arm tightly, she screamed at me. "Now say out loud, 'I am going to get my head cut off so that I cannot ever wet the bed again.'"

I cried hysterically. Irene begged, "Momma, please give her one more chance. Just one more." But Mrs. Lilla held me down with her foot, and twisted my neck down sideways onto the block of wood. I held my breath until I blacked out, waiting for the ax to fall.

When Papa got home, Lily, who was twelve, told him what had happened. He picked me up in his arms, rocking, gathering up my little sister, Susie, too, and glared at his

1

new wife, his face contorted with rage: "Get gone fast! If you're here at noon, I'll be back to shoot you."

As soon as he rode off on his horse, Mrs. Lilla and her two daughters, Irene and Lily, stuffed everything into sheets — pots and pans, clothes, even Papa's and my clothes, then loaded it all onto a hand-pulled wagon. She left me and Susie, who was only two, alone in that shanty in the piney woods. When Papa got home for lunch, he found us there alone.

"She took all my clothes," I said.

"Show me which way Mrs. Lilla and the girls took." I pointed, and Papa quickly lifted us onto the horse and mounted, Susie behind him, with me clutching her from behind. As he rode down the dirt path, suddenly the little black and white spotted feist, our hunting dog, darted out from the bushes, barking.

"Whoa, Mary!" Papa called out. "We are going to find our stuff here." Sure enough, when we were all down from the horse, Fido led right to the place where all bedclothes, the cooking utensils, and clothes were hidden.

I stared down that curving dirt road with tall black pine trees shoulder to shoulder on either side and begged Papa ,"Can we go look for my real Mother now?"

Papa picked both Susie and me back up onto the horse, and walked beside it, holding us on, tears trickling down his cheeks. "My poor little motherless chillen," he said over and over. "My poor little motherless chillen."

Our real mother, Rose, was a Seminole Indian, with skin golden as a sunset, a high cheek-boned face, luminous eyes, and a lilting laugh she used often. She wore a long, shiny braid down her back and white dresses with blue, red and yellow rickrack dancing around the full skirts. As she and my grandmother Susie James washed clothes in a tub outside her chickee on the Croom-Choo-Chee reservation, their laughter echoed while we played in the abandoned phosphate mine near the railroad track.

Grandma was known for her moonshine recipe: Mash corn, add a little round flower called Hall, very sweet and good, then elderberries if you can find them, stir in wood alcohol that could kill you stone dead, and pour in a little Sterno. Grandma Susie had made herself a still of barrel staves and crockery. Sometimes people on the reservation would drink raw Sterno heat that could almost knock your head off. But before the government refused to allow any Indians to buy cans of Sterno, the tribe people got together and loved it.

Our clapboard house on the reservation overflowed with children. Mama's first husband, James Cox, had been killed when a train broadsided the mule wagon he was driving. They had two daughters, Louise (Lula), fourteen , and Dorothy (Dora), twelve. To marry Rose, Curtis James McClary had to convert from Baptist to Catholic; all the Seminoles were Catholic. Twin brothers, Robert (Bubba) and William (Buddy) came along in 1911, then more twins, Jacques (Jack) and me (called Tannie because of my dark brown skin) born January 7, 1913. Susie was a year and a half younger, and Minnie just a baby with Mama expecting her third set of twins that summer I was three.

When our mother's sister arrived to help out, I had on a little brown corduroy coat—and nothing else underneath. Mother was washing clothes in a tub in the yard as the train stopped for water. When she saw Big Baby get off, Mama picked up Minnie in one arm and Susie in the other and headed for the train. I was so mad she left me on the front porch that I threw that coat off, and began to run behind her, screaming at the top of my lungs, a fat— very fat— little nature-girl, weighing as much as my two little sisters put together. I had learned early on that if I screamed for attention, somebody would give me a sugar-tit (from the cane fields) to suck. So I made sure others had ample opportunities to shut me up with candy. With me around, poor Jacques never had a chance to develop much of a personality. He stayed placid, always smiling, never scheming like his twin sister — me!

When Mother and Aunt Baby left to go fishing, she told Lula and Dora, "Don't have any boys at this house while I'm away." But soon I overheard Lula ordering someone to go to mother's chicken yard and get two hens to cook for Keiser and Luke.

"Give old tattler big girl all she can eat so that she don't tell Mama," Lula said.

Of course, I took three helpings of everything, then ran down to a little homemade bridge across a ditch to wait for our mother. I leapt into her arms, knocking the fishing pole and pail askew in my hurry to report, "Mama, guess what! Dora and Lula killed and cooked your chickens for their boyfriends."

"Didn't they give you any?"

"No," I pouted. "None at all."

"Just wait 'til I get home. I'll fix those two young ladies!" (That was fine until the next day. Dora spanked me so long and so hard with a switch that I never tattled on my big sisters again.)

Lula and Dora looked like Seminoles with the gold hues and straight noses of our mother and grandmother Susie. Our grandfather, Eugene Alonzo James, was a descendent of a pre-historic tribe, a dark-skinned, medium-height people who inhabited Florida long before the Spanish came. Some historians believe them to be Indians, while others have alluded to them as "Africans" who occupied Florida from the period around 450 AD.

Papa was just twelve years-old, an orphan who'd never had a chance for an education, when the recruiters lured him and other young Black boys from the Sea Islands of South Carolina to the west coast of Florida with the promise of jobs in the phosphate mines. But the adolescents found hell instead: fourteen hours of work seven days a week under the point of a gun with food and primitive shelter the only pay. Then he was stolen by another man who owned a sawmill in Brooksville, near Croom-ChooChee. For the first time in his life, he was hated and considered stupid because of his dark color and his language that people in Florida couldn't understand: Gullah.

Gullah was the language made famous in Uncle Remus stories with "b'rer" meaning brother, "gwine" for going to, "een" for in. Gullah coined the word "buckra," which means white man. McClary pronounced Annie as "Ah-ni", the same way he'd say "Ah declare," according to Dr.

Walker. The lowest class Blacks who speak Gullah were called "Geechees."

The language was a mixture of African tongues that had developed among the slaves brought to the group of islands off the coast of South Carolina to work on cotton plantations. The people as well as the language were known as Gullah. H.L. Mencken once called Gullah "the only American dialect unintelligible to persons from other parts of the country."

Worse, social scientists assumed Gullah was spoken "because of social backwardness, isolation, simple-mindedness and physiological inferiority." One widely-published account by Ambrose Gonzales, who edited a number of volumes of Gullah, was particularly damning: "Slovenly and careless of speech, these Gullahs seized upon the peasant English used by some of the early settlers and by the white servants of the wealthier colonists, wrapped their clumsy tongues about it as well as they could, and enriched with certain expressive African words, it issued through their flat noses and thick lips as so workable a form of speech that it was gradually adopted by the other slaves and became in time the accepted Negro speech of the lower districts of South Carolina and Georgia." Not until halfway through the twentieth century did anthropologists discover most Gullah words—and the name Gullah--came from the Umbundu dialect of Angola. (Wade-Lewis)

But the culture itself bequeathed a rare gift: "African customs and images were kept alive by nightly storytelling as 'liars' began to spin their yarns to two generations of Gullah children," according to anthropologist John Smith.

The liar was an itinerant, usually an older male who moved from one former plantation settlement to another, spinning animal tales (Uncle Remus, for example) and mortality tales in exchange for food and shelter. Gullah culture began with transfer of slaves from Africa, focusing on how isolation factors preserved African culture and a unique language, which is similar to Cajun English.

Even though they spoke Gullah, Papa's two grandmothers had been shipped via the Royal African Company as slave cargo from Jamaica, West Indies, after having gone through the "Breaking On" period there. But both of Papa's parents, Dollie and Adolphus, were McClarys from birth, the son and daughter of two Black slave women and the white McClary brothers who owned the plantations.

Papa's parents were freed three years before he was born, and died when he was three. He and his blind sister, Lavinia, Lizzie Brown (who later became famous), Van, and Charles moved from Goose Creek, South Carolina, to live with a cousin, Maggie Duke near Charleston. She was rather like the character in the nursery rhyme: "There was an old woman who lived in a shoe/ with so many children she didn't know what to do./ So she gave them all broth without any bread and spanked them all soundly and sent them to bed."

My father, Curtis James McClary, was humble, but he prided himself on his parents' strength during slavery. Like many slaves, he told us children, his mother wore over-sized skirts with big aprons. They would sing spirituals like "Carry Me Back to Old Virginny," a signal for the slaves to crawl from one woman's skirt to the next as they escaped to the underground railroad. My father told the stories proudly, but constantly preached to his children "This is the reason I want you to go to school and get a good education. Then you won't have to go through all the pain and suffering by the buckra."

My parents hoped that a move to the Tomoka Land Company Turpentine Camp in 1911 would be a chance for a better life. Jacques and I and the younger children were born there. But the struggle to survive was tragic. Within the next few years the unsanitary conditions resulted in death for three members of our family.

The Buncombie Hill turpentine camp was typical of the approximately 1,000 camps in the Deep South. The camp where we were produced turpentine and rosin and had about 50 to 75 people working at times of full production.

Papa's job was chipping at the old pine trees with thick bark. It seemed to me he walked a hundred miles a day to chop boxes. Papa would hack first from the right, then from the left to make a v shape called a "cat face." From the V, sap would run down a metal thing into a rust-colored clay cup which was fastened to the tree with a nail. The iron hack tool he carried over his shoulder was very heavy. He walked awfully bent-over one-sided from the weight.

The great pine forests of Florida contributed products of value to marine commerce for nearly two centuries before sawmills made their appearance. The first products were pitch and tar produced from the sap of the pine tree. They were called "naval stores" because carpenters used them to caulk the seams of wooden ships. The present products of pine tree sap – turpentine and rosin – are still known by that name.

With the advent of iron ships, chemical research found new uses for the pine gums. Turpentine now thins the paint that colors our houses and it is used extensively in the manufacture of polishes, perfume bases, waterproof cement and for various medicinal purposes.

Rosin, once discarded as a practically valueless by- product of turpentine, is today the principal ingredient of the varnish that covers floors and furniture. It is also used in the manufacture of soap, insulating material, writing paper, printing ink, sealing wax, plastics and linoleum.

Sometimes men came with wagons pulled by mules. They collected the raw gum from the pots and took the sticky pitch to a still for refining. Some men came with wagons pulled by teams of long-eared mules to collect the raw gum from the pots, and then they rode to the refining still. However, Papa was often in fear of his life while tramping through the snake and alligator-infested swampy woods. The feared white "woods riders" on horseback would sometimes descend suddenly on Papa and other workers and accuse them of not working fast enough or not paying up debts at the commissary. I often wondered if Papa would shoot those men because they struck him with whips and treated him so cruelly.

Men were often whipped or beaten to death. According to the *Florida History Network*, "the local sheriff would be in league with the owners of the turpentine companies who would pay the defendants' court fines, get them released from jail, and force them to pay off the fines by working in squalid, barbarous conditions." After the *New York World* newspaper reported "prisoners [were] dying after repeated and daily whippings," the legislature was forced to investigate. That wasn't easy because owners of the companies were usually politically connected."

The camp owner, Archie Clark, who was red-headed and hot-tempered, talked down to the men as if they were children. He compelled all the men to buy everything at the commissary. They'd order a side of bacon, five pounds of dried lima beans and so forth. When they got their checks at the end of the month, Mr. Archie would go over to the black ledger. There were always overcharges. The men couldn't read, so they had to depend on the owner's word. By the time the accounting was finished, the men would earn just $4 or $5 a week. It was just like after slavery, when black people had to still work on the farm.

In 1891, the Florida legislature passed a law that said debt was a crime if the workers stopped working before the debt was paid. Some workers just fell deeply into debt and could not leave. The turpentine camps seemed to be the worst places, so much so that President Theodore Roosevelt had noted some jobs as being a form of slavery.

Blacks were treated in much the same way as before 1865. White employers and officials went after missing blacks and arrested them, under protection of vagrancy laws, using whatever force felt necessary to protect the financial investment. The worker had to stay with the employer until his debt was paid or "face criminal charges that made him liable to the convict lease, often being led to the same man from whom he had tried to escape," it was reported in the *Journal of Forest History.*

Our family couldn't even afford smoked bacon. The food supply we got was mostly fatback (they called white bacon), and dried peas and beans or other dried, preserved foods, and corn meal. I saw my father ask for money for shoes and food. Mr. Clark looked at the book and told him, "Jim, you don't have anything coming. You owe me." That commissary was based on the sharecropping system. Papa walked out with tears in his eyes, needing money so badly to buy food for the family.

School wasn't easy to come by since compulsory education was mandated only for white children in the state of Florida. Nobody in the turpentine camp went to school, and no education was available at the camp. But my father got his cousin's wife, Mary McLeod Bethune, who had founded the Daytona Educational and Industrial Training School for Negro Girls in nearby Daytona Beach in 1904, to come out by mule-drawn wagon to teach basic reading and arithmetic to my mother, Rose. She and the four oldest children learned basic numbers and how to read a little, even though Papa could neither read nor write himself.

"I want you children never to live this kind of life," Papa preached, "never to have to take foolishness from the white man. He has always looked out for his interest, so you will have to look out for yours. And you can't do it without education."

With no running water or electricity, few people were able to keep clean. The shanties had cracks and holes which allowed rats, roaches, even snakes inside. Yards were bare dirt, which blew in through the wall and floor cracks. Infections and viruses ran rampant, but no doctor was available to help black people.

My mother went back to Croom Coo Chee to give birth to the last set of twins, her ninth and tenth children. Before dawn [on July 17, 1916], someone called the midwife to deliver the babies. The temperature inside was stifling in the clapboard shack. My mother had struggled all day and night for a difficult breach delivery with only a mid-wife to help. Because of the rough handling and non-sterile conditions, she developed childbed fever [an infection of the endometrium and bloodstream]. At 10 to 7 in the morning, Eugene and Jesse were delivered still-born. My mother died at 4:10 that afternoon. Rose McClary was just 27 years-old.

I watched the women in her family bathe her with water brought in from a well in buckets, then dress her in the ritual white robe while the men took rough pine boards and hammered together a crude box. They put a full Indian headdress on my mother's head and a crucifix in her fingers. Then they placed her and the two babies together into the unpainted box and lifted it onto a mule-drawn wagon. We children watched it go down the road, followed by a procession of adults on horseback and mule-drawn wagons to make the journey to the Seminole burial grounds near Dade City.

As the ruling tribe elder, Grandmother Susie got to decide where the children were to live—which meant we never got to stay together as a family again. Aunt Minnie took the baby who was named for her (but nicknamed "Rat"). Lula and Dora stayed with Grandma Susie, and the three boys went to their mother's brother, Uncle Charlie and Aunt Jill (Josephine) James. Grandmother also wanted Susie, since she was named for her. Nobody wanted me, the only child in the family with dark brown skin—except Papa. Since he thought I would be lonely, he refused to let Susie leave him either. The three of us went back to the turpentine camp to live.

So before I was four, I became the woman of the house in charge of my two and a half year-old sister. When Papa would go off to work and leave us, he put up dried beans to soak overnight. In the morning, he told me to keep wood on a low-burning flame. I dutifully attended to the beans or peas and added water, and I saw to it that the stove had wood in it, and even baked sweet potatoes in the oven part.

I had watched my father make corn bread, so one day I decided to surprise him with my cooking. The beans were done with the fatback and the potatoes in them. The grits were made. So when he came home, he saw that I had made cornbread so brown and beautiful. He picked me up and swung me around. "Baby, where did you learn to cook?" I said I had watched him. He sat down, took one bite, began to choke, and tears ran out of his eyes. "Oh, honey, you put in Perline (detergent)," he said.

I cried, worried I had poisoned him. "No, don't feel bad and be sorry," he soothed me. "You were trying to copy from your Papa to make me happy. That can never be wrong." So then he showed me the right ingredients: cornmeal, baking powder, and salt. From then on, I made it just fine.

The neighbor lady, Mrs. Arlyss, showed me how to unravel muslin flour sacks to save the thread, then wind it around paper for crocheting. She'd come over in the morning to make us hot grits, then stay to crochet covers for orange crate tables—and everything else in the house. By four, I crocheted, too.

One day Papa came home for lunch to find me sitting on a rusty metal milk crate behind the shanty. I was crocheting and crying as I tried in vain to untangle the threads. He picked me up from the crate and pressed me close. "Baby, why are you crying?"

"Because my mother is dead," I said, now sobbing hysterically. "I miss her, and I want to die to be with her."

My father sat down on the crate, cradling me like an infant. "Baby, if you die, Papa will be very hurt and lonely, so please don't wish to leave me. Besides, you are one wise child who is going to be a teacher." On that promise, I still felt sad, but I decided it was important to live after all. Papa needed me. Besides I had something important to do.

After that Papa brought Susie and me to a neighbor, Mrs. Boyd, the mid-wife, so that someone would take care of us. The only problem was eleven year-old Minnie Boyd, who'd been the baby of the family and spoiled by her father. Now Susie and I were getting some of the attention. So when Mr. Boyd went to work and Mrs. Boyd left to run errands or deliver a baby, Minnie would come out with the switch. "Dance the jig," she'd order me, stinging my legs with the switch, forcing me to dance until my legs were red with welts. Minnie threatened that if we told anyone about the beatings, she would kill both Susie and me. So we never breathed a word to anyone.

Papa tried right away to find a replacement for our mother, but he said he'd never marry a woman with skin as dark as his. One Black woman he knew suspected him of running out on her, so she set a trap. She filled a pail with liquid lye and attached it by a string to the door frame. When Papa came through the door, the pail emptied on him, by sheer luck ruining his coat instead of his skin and eyes. After that, Papa said, he was convinced all Black women had evil in them.

"But what about me?" I would ask. "I'm as dark as you."

"Baby, you're one of a kind. You're so special! Nobody else will ever be like you," he'd reply. I never heard him say even one negative thing about me as long as he lived.

Being so special, I imagined Papa didn't need another wife. Sure enough, even though he married Mrs. Lilla, she was booted out right away when she was mean to me. The marriage lasted only a few weeks. I couldn't imagine anybody more evil than Mrs. Lilla — until the next stepmother arrived a few months later. For both the new wife and me, now almost six years old, it was hate at first sight. At second sight, I took a gun and tried to kill her.

Life with 'Mrs. Ill Treatment'

Not only was my next stepmother, Missy, an alcoholic but, unlike me, she was skinny and walked bow-legged. She switched when she walked. Because her rear end was flat, she'd wear a stinking old pad to make artificial buttocks. She'd open that mouth with the two gold teeth right in front and call me at age six "a big ass nigger." Since Missy's skin color was what used to be called "high yeller," she felt superior. But I never knew Missy to take even one bath in years. The odor warned people of her presence.

Every morning she gagged, which is how I knew she was waking up. She hit the floor with a force to stagger across the room to drink moonshine as I lay there, holding my breath, my heart beating so hard I could hear it, waiting, listening, thinking of what I could do when Missy called, remembering the decapitation attempt by Mrs. Lilla. I had dreams of running away. But where? What would Papa do if I left? What would become of Susie?

Missy would go out in the mornings to "bust suds" for a well-known white family on North Street, leaving us little girls to fend for ourselves. The Cliftons, who had hogs and cows, would go around selling fresh meats, milk, and illegal moonshine. Missy would get her share of the moonshine, and stagger home, reeking of it, waving oak switches in her hand, rocking from side to side.

"Susie! Annie Mae, git over here!" she'd call out as soon as got within earshot of the house. She'd take off her shoes at the door and come after us. When we spied her, we hid under the house, which sat on stacks of concrete blocks. We'd crawl from the back to the front and back again. It never occurred to Missy to look under the house. But when we finally did show our faces at suppertime, our stepmother would whip us with oak switches for no apparent reason at all.

One day Susie and I heard some women talking— Mrs. White and Mrs. Thomas and Mrs. Howard from next door. "Lord, one of these days when those children are going to grow up," said Mrs. White, "they'll beat that woman and not take any more beatings from her."

Susie said to me, "And that day might be tomorrow." As quiet and pious as Susie was at age five, she'd say, "Tannie, I love to fight." Sure enough, Susie got hold of Missy's switch and hit her repeatedly on the thighs. From that day, Missy never hit Susie again, just me who wouldn't talk back. Even I was afraid of Susie. Little sister bossed everybody around. But Papa saw her as a placid child, "just like her mother, a shame-faced woman."

I often wondered if Papa really knew how lonely and sad I was. Certainly he, or nobody else for that matter, could judge the seriousness of this condition from outward appearances. I still greeted others and with a ready smile and usually a warm and loving embrace. Thus Papa used to say, "Dat child is a wonderful person. She loves people— she is happy!" But this statement could be equated with the words of an old African-American folk-Blues song: "Baby, you don't know; Baby, you don't know; Baby, you don't

17

know my mind. When you see me laughing, I'm laughing just to keep from crying; laughing, I won't lose my mind."

I was always interested in doing something. I used pampas grass with long roots. I'd wash it off, braid the hair, then take crepe paper and make a beautiful dress. The longer the hair, the more you appreciated it. My father wouldn't let any one of us cut our hair — nor straighten it. "God gave you the kind of hair He wanted you to have — so keep it that way."

What did interest me was what my twin brother and the other boys did. I would show them how to take burlap and make little tents to roast marshmallows and hot dogs. But the boys got mad because I told them just what to do step by step. It seemed unfair that they got to strip off their clothes and go for a swim, so I stripped, too. When my brother saw me standing naked, he chased me home and told my father how ashamed he was of me. My father didn't smack me, but he said, "Remember, you're developing, and your brothers are ashamed."

My father said, "Don't have contact with people who can have a bad influence on you." Unfortunately, that included my Aunt Minnie, who was an alcoholic. So my job was to take care of my sister, Minnie. I didn't dare be bad. This was the state of affairs with me. Perhaps, deep down inside of me, there was the notion that, although this loneliness and sadness I felt was present during the "nighttime" years of my growing up, a ray of light would appear to brighten up things during the darkest part of the night.

Only Papa, who worshipped me, made these times bearable — he really did. Every day he'd say, "That's a bright child. She's smart. She's going to be a teacher."

Every day my stepmother would call me "a stupid, ugly nigger," predicting, "You'll never get a man 'cause you'll still wet the bed," and "by the time you're 12, you won't be able to see your shoes for your (pregnant) belly," or "you're as mean as your cussed old daddy."

When I was six, Papa moved from the turpentine camp to town at the suggestion of Mary McLeod Bethune, who agreed she would start the school's first kindergarten class so I could have a place to go and learn. South Carolina Gullah-born, too, she adored "Brother Jim" as she always called him. She'd left her husband, Papa's cousin, Mr. Bethune, alone in South Carolina when she felt God was calling her to Daytona Beach to start a school for Negro girls, which she founded with $1.50 and five little girls (plus her own son, Albert, 5). They had to clear out the city dump, known as "Hell's Hole" to build the school in 1904.

By the time I started kindergarten in 1920, more than a hundred young girls combined learning to read and count with domestic training on raising gardens, washing clothes and sewing. I already knew the domestic chores, so I worked on schoolwork until bedtime every night. I loved Mrs. Bethune—loved her like a substitute mother.

I didn't want to talk like Papa because I wanted to sound educated. I spent a year in kindergarten, but only two weeks in first grade, and one-half semester in second grade. Within a year and a half, I had been "promoted" all the way to third grade. But being always the youngest in my class left me isolated and more lonely. The other girls hated me for being young but making all A's in school, so when I'd approach, they'd say, "Go away, baby, and get your bottle."

I found a way to gain acceptance and be like them. At eight, I started smoking cigarettes—a habit that would hold me hostage for the next 70 years.

I usually sat on the steps and smoked while I watched other children play, but I would have something to read or do that was creative. So I considered myself sort of anti-social. I thought I was better than they because I was doing something intellectual.

I was sewing all my own clothes and Susie's, too, using my most treasured possession, my real mother's old treadle sewing machine. Papa would send me down to the feed store to get a dozen muslin bags for 10 cents, then to the drug store to get dye, and old newspaper pieces to create my own patterns. One sack would make a shirt, another a blouse. I'd make blouses and skirts for my friends. Soon other children were clamoring to pay 25 cents or 50 cents for new clothes, enough for me to get thread and—once a year— two bolts of real yard goods. From that, I even made pleated skirts. The machine was the one real joy in my life.

But one day when I came home, the machine was not there. Missy had taken the machine left to me by my mother and traded it in for one for herself. When I saw it, I screamed. "That's not my machine!" That day I knew I would have killed Missy if I could have got near a gun. Instead, tears running down my cheeks, inconsolable over the loss of my only possession, I grabbed my stepmother by both arms. "How dare you take my machine? Papa said this was just for me. How could you? How could you?" And then I slapped her.

When Susie heard Missy scream, she took over. Susie beat her to a pulp and told her to go get my machine back. But she didn't, and we concluded it wouldn't do any good to let Papa know. I didn't want Papa to have to suffer my own hurt—so he never even noticed the old machine had been replaced, and Missy, of course, kept mum.

I swallowed my hurt and intense hate for my stepmother, deciding I'd get back at Missy by proving her wrong about me. At the same time, I felt very sorry for Papa.

I never reported abuse by the stepmothers because I was afraid that if Papa got word people were messing around with his children, he would kill them and go to jail for the rest of his life, and then I wouldn't have either parent. As young as I was, that's the burden I felt I had to carry.

At age eight, I was forced to scrub all the floors at home. We had a huge square grand piano that sat on four legs. Knowing how badly I wanted to play, Papa bought it down the street for $15 when Mrs. Johnson's son got married. I was on my hands and knees scrubbing when Missy came in drunk and started telling me how stupid I was, just like my real mother--a "savage," she said, and added my mother had been "playing the dozens." Then she commanded that I do the whole floor over. "You missed a place right over there and made this all motley."

"Yes I did!" I talked back for the first time. Playing the dozens (talking bad about your mother) was bad for the black side, and it was equally bad for the Indian side to be called a savage. So I jumped off my knees. Back then shotguns were put on racks over every door to protect the houses. So I got a chair and pulled up and got that gun. I shot toward her. Missy was high on moonshine, but not too high to run. I followed her with the heavy gun. Boom! Boom!

Mr. Ashley, who lived in back, heard the shooting, so he jumped the fence and ran in. "Mae, what are you doing?"

"She called my mother a savage, and I'm going to kill her," I said. "She deserves to be shot."

The neighbor took one look at the slobbering, drunken Missy and quietly took the gun and led me over to his house.

Soon Susie came over and asked, "Tannie, do you want me to go back over there and beat her up?"

"No, are you going to tell Papa?"

"Mr. Ashley said we have to," said Susie. "Why not?"

"Because then Papa would kill her, and you and I would have no one."

Missy would go to bed with anyone to get more money for Moonshine. Susie caught her with one of the Cliftons and told on her to Papa. But I said, "No, this didn't happen. Susie's just making it up."

Susie took me aside. "Tannie, you know how many times this has happened." Of course, I did. But I again was thinking of Papa. I couldn't afford to take the risk of him being taken away for killing her. All Papa did was smack Missy for getting drunk.

The McClarys, like all Blacks in Daytona Beach, lived on the "wrong side" of the canal, in Midway, which meant children had to go all the way into Kingston, which was white, for the mail. The white children used to meet at the canal divide and throw rocks and call us "niggers." So Susie, Thelma, Abby, Lucille, and I would start building up an arsenal on Sunday afternoon to defend ourselves. We had a big rock bed to prepare for the assault.

As we girls approached the canal, Annie Mae Clifton would call out, "Here come the niggers!" And the rocks would fly.

Then Susie would retort, "Here come the niggers, and here come the stupid Crackers we're going to fight!"

Then rocks hurled from the other side, and children started running and scattered. Sometimes a child would get hit in the foot, but nobody really got hurt. When we went back from the mail, everything was all right, and Annie Mae Clifton and I spent the night together making doll clothes.

That's the kind of relationship the races had in Daytona. The whites lived on the east side of the railroad tracks toward the ocean, and the blacks on the west. Blacks had separate express deliverymen, their own postmen, and even their own policemen. Black police could never go across the tracks to arrest a white person. White police usually didn't cross the tracks to come get a black unless he was a real desperado. But that principle of protection didn't apply when the Ku Klux Klan was involved.

One night Papa shot a thousand KKK. Or at least that's the way I told the story in first grade. My father had told us that Mr. Booker (our neighbor) had worked as a farm hand for a man in Osteen. After harvesting, the man asked for his pay. Instead the landowner knocked him down and said he didn't pay niggers, whereupon Mr. Booker grabbed the shovel and beat up the man, then ran. He had a sheriff's posse looking for him.

In those days, the prisoner usually didn't make it all the thirty miles from Daytona to the County Seat in DeLand for trial. Lynch mobs strung the black man up along the way. So there wasn't any question about expecting the law to be fair. Mr. Booker was lucky that a white person took him in, a member of the Masonic Lodge, a Christian brotherhood of which McClary was a member. The white man called Papa, who loaded up his truck with sugar cane stalks, then hid Mr. Booker underneath the crop to bring him back to the McClary house.

It wasn't long before Sheriff Jimmy Derden came knocking at the McClary's front door. "Hey, Jim. You got Mr. Booker here?"

"I ain't goin' to say he is—or ain't," Papa replied. "But I will say this much. You cannot come over my threshold. This is my house and my pant legs are just as long as yours. And another thing. I don't call you Jimmy—so you can call me by my proper name."

"What's that?" Derden was mad.

"Deacon James McClary," Papa said. After that, everybody in town, black and white alike, called him "Deac."

Even though the sheriff left, the men knew the trouble was just beginning. Sure enough, about dark a neighbor came running to our house with the news he'd heard a whole bunch of horses coming down the road to the house. All the families in the neighborhood rushed to the McClary's. Papa ordered all the women and children to hide under tables at the back of the house. Then the women doused the lanterns while the men and big boys armed themselves with 12-gauge, eight-shell pump shotguns and waited.

Papa gave directions: "Wait quiet 'til they stop in front and I give the signal." From my position, hugging Susie under the kitchen table, I heard a thousand hoofs. Through the side window, we children could see the lighted torches and white sheets of the riders.

"Now!" Papa's shout was followed by more booms than 100 thunderbolts. A torch of fire landed in the front room through the window.

"Get a bucket!" one man shouted. I did, and threw it on the flame. The fire was out, but I could hear tortured screams of men who were shot out in front of the house.

"Oh, Lawd! Lawd!" Women's voices anguished with their fear. But when the horses left and the house was quiet again, not one man inside the house was dead. I couldn't sleep that night, worried they might come back and kill everybody.

Pretty soon Papa came in to see how I was and to comfort me. "People who are racist and do bad things against other people are very insecure," he said. "They don't like themselves and take to blaming others for their lot in life.

Even the KKK. You just remember that all people are made good in God's image. Some of his children just go astray. But let God deal with them. Don't you try to judge them."

Even so Papa had to stay on guard for his life. I worried that Papa might shoot some of those white men when he went into Daytona Beach—because whenever he loaded the wagon with his children to go to town, he dressed up in his Sunday suit, but then put on starched and ironed overalls (with suspenders) and a denim jumper over his suit. Then he stuck his 38 special or 45 Colt in between his suit and jumper.

Blacks didn't own cars, but they weren't allowed to ride buses, so they had to use black taxi drivers. But even this wasn't safe after what happened to Mr. Snell. He'd gone over to the white neighborhood to pick up Miss Lannie Johnson, who cleaned by day for the Brubakers. As he was driving down the street, he heard a crash, and saw one of the Brubaker's kids and his bike fly out across the hood of his car.

Frantic, Snell made the mistake of knocking on white doors to try to get some help for the child. Immediately the Sheriff's crew came out to take him to DeLand to arraign him. He never got there. White men got up a posse and killed Snell on the spot.

Papa was thrifty and knowledgeable, even though he couldn't read or write. He was always busy doing something to earn a living—following crops in season, finding used lumber to build frames and screen wire to make windows. One storeowner bragged, "Mr. McClary can tell you down to five nails how many it takes to build a house."

I was especially proud of this, because I'd been giving him lessons. I was eight years old, in the third grade, when Papa did the grading of US 1 south from Daytona to New Smyrna Beach, using a mule team, pans and shovels.

I organized night school for the men construction workers and taught them to read and write. They had to come for one hour Monday through Thursday nights for the charge of 50 cents a week. With the money, I bought pencils, papers, and slates, and gave each man a project to do. Papa's was to build a house out of matches. He even created partitions for that house. It wasn't like our real house—the house of matches had an indoor bathroom.

I had wanted so badly to learn to play the piano, so at age nine I went down the street and asked Miss Harris if she would teach me. When she told me the cost was 50 cents a lesson, twice a week, I had to tell her I couldn't afford it. But she said, if I'd come on Saturday and scrub her kitchen floor and rake her dirt yard, she'd give me free lessons. After only four lessons, I told her I wanted to play for the Sunday school at my father's church—and I did. I didn't want to have to learn to play all those sharps in the hymns, so I just changed them all to flats. Nobody seemed to notice, and I went on playing.

Papa was taken out and beaten by white men when I was nine. He and a man named Thornton Smith were referred to as "Damn Niggers." He supported a councilman named Mr. Armstrong, and Papa used to recruit voters. When it was time for election, Armstrong would give Papa money to buy a whole hog for a barbecue. The next day, Papa would throw a picnic open to anyone in the community. As many whites as blacks would attend, but segregation was still the order of the day every other day. When blacks got their very first park on Cypress Street, right off Nova Road, the blacks always referred to it as McClary Park.

Even boys who used to shoot craps would stop when they'd spy my father and call out, "Here comes Deac." And they'd throw down the dice and run. He didn't allow any congregating on street corners. He'd walk with a crooked cane and use the horn to grab a child and talk to him about getting to school. "Ain't no such thing as delinquency," Papa would say, "just parents who not doin' their job!"

My father was not literate, but he knew how to limn a hymn, teach Sunday school and do a prayer. He was a 32nd degree Mason. He could recite that six or seven-page document for the ceremony by heart. He was also a carpenter who knew how to tell—within five nails—how many nails were needed for a whole house. Papa had four rental houses he'd built himself. You see, we had 10 rooms. My father was a very handy man, a self-educated carpenter and plumber. He made cinder blocks to sell for five cents apiece. Our house was on Walnut Street. He built houses to rent, about $3.50 a week in the early 20's.

In the summertime he went to Pittsburgh to work in the steel industry, and in winter to Fort Pierce to work in the pineapple business, anywhere he could find a crop to pick or a job to do. Missy never worked because Papa didn't believe in women working—except for me. I had to be exceptional in every way. To him, I was the Queen of the Universe.

My papa, like Mrs. Bethune, had white friends who respected him highly. White pharmacists, white grocers, and a white doctor were loyal. His credit was good anywhere. He could send any of us to get something from a store, and they would write it on a ledger. Then when my Papa got paid, he would pay them. They all called him Deacon McClary. So I guess that's why we didn't grow up with any fight back.

To say he was religious was an understatement. To keep the promise he made when marrying my mother, we went to 6 a.m. mass every Sunday at St. Paul's Catholic Church on Ridgewood Avenue. Then we'd come home for Papa's breakfast Bible reading.

He operated on the sayings: "Take what you have. Make what you need." His slogan was "Let every knock be a boost." He told us to be determined to go even higher. He made a habit, both in prayer and lecture, of teaching us how to live and to ignore bad examples. He read Matthew 5: "Blessed are the meek..." He told us how slaves, through prayer and endurance and fortitude, could say, "I know, Lord."

"Speaking of how white people hate us," I told Papa one Sunday morning after early mass, "have you noticed that we have to sit at the back of the church, but we drink from the communion cup first, then the whites have to drink after us? If they think we're dirty, how come they do that?"

Papa just laughed. "You one wise child. You notice things they haven't figured out yet."

After Papa's breakfast sermon at home, I went to Methodist services at school. Then he became one of the founders of the Greater Friendship Baptist Church in Daytona. So the Baptists baptized father and he became a deacon. My father would go to the Bible and tell me, "Jesus said, 'turn the other cheek.' Let them have both cheeks to slap. I don't want to see my children killed. I don't want any of you girls to have to scrub buckra's floors. If you have to do that to get money for school, just remember: this is the means, not the end. Think of your end as being a professional somewhere doing something to better people. With every stroke of that mop, you say: 'This is just the means. This is just the means. This is not an end.' You laugh at their attitudes. Keep in mind they are insecure. Remember, if they don't love themselves, they can't love anybody else."

The big problem for me was that Papa ignored Missy's examples. He couldn't see the evil in her. But I wanted "every knock to be a boost" out the door for her. Instead Papa banished my sister Lula for committing the ultimate sin: "meeting paydays."

Lula, who was 11 years older than me, used it against me that she had scoliosis and said it was because she didn't have any childhood. She claimed my mother hadn't allowed her to play with other children, because I wouldn't go with anybody else but my father and Lula. Jack, my twin, would stay with anybody, but if Lula attempted to leave me for a minute, she claimed, I would cry and yell, "I want Lula." And so, she said, that deprived her of her childhood and friends. She said I caused her to be deformed because she used to have to carry the big fat me around. However, every one of the girls in my mother's family, including me, have had twisted spines.

Lula always referred to herself as being very pretty, and so did everyone. You'd think so, too. She was not dark brown like me, but a beautiful light gold tint, with facial features like my mother, a thin straight nose and high cheekbones. Everyone called her "Lula, the Indian girl."

Can you see the difference between her and Mae the South Carolinian with black skin, a flat nose, and wide lips? When Lula got angry, she'd call me "old black thing." That was a fighting word in those days. So I'd yell, "Papa, she called me..." I didn't have to say any more. That did it. I didn't have to tell him the rest of the sentence.

He'd answer. "That's all right, Baby. The blacker the berry, the sweeter the juice." Another thing he'd say was "Blacker is wonderful." It was very common in the black community to talk about shit color. When she called black, I'd call her "old shit color." That would shut her up for a while.

She earned money, but when I once, when I was six, asked her for a nickel for a composition book, she said "Hell, no! Go out and work!" I cried and cried.

At 15, Lula became a prostitute. She'd go to the turpentine camp on paydays. The prostitution went against my father's belief. He told her she was not welcome at his house. Then he told us never to speak to her or about her again.

Until now, every grown-up woman I'd known was evil – except my dead mother, of course. In my miserable childhood, I didn't dream I was about to get close to two real ladies, who not only changed my life: these two women changed the whole United States of America.

Mama Mame

and the 'Big Shots'

Unlike the women who later became my friends, Toni Morrison (*Beloved*) and Maya Angelou (*I Know Why the Caged Bird Sings*), I never wanted to look like Shirley Temple. I never had a desire to be white. Maybe Toni and Maya were more privileged than I, but more likely it's because my father and Mary McLeod Bethune, whom I always called Mama Mame, instilled a sense of pride in the value of Blackness. I loved her—loved her like a substitute mother.

She used to come to the turpentine camp, where I was born, on Saturdays to teach the people how to read and write. She had persuaded my father to move to Daytona Beach so she could put me in school.

She and my father called each other brother and sister. Not only was she related to him by marriage to his cousin, but my maternal grandmother, Susie, was married to Mrs. Bethune's uncle, James McLeod. Mama Mame and Papa liked to tease each other. They both had extremely dark skin and liked to dress to the teeth.

Once she and my father and the Reverend Barkeley were walking down the street in Jacksonville and somebody said, "Here come the kings and a queen from Africa." So on the Sunday afternoon programs before the Rockefellers, Gambles, and the like, she'd call out, "Stand up, Brother McClary. Let these people in Daytona Beach see a king from Africa." My father would just howl.

The influence Mrs. Bethune had on all of us was because of her treatment to students. Her "title" was always Mother to students, faculty, and townspeople. In all the years I was around them, I never heard either her or my father use the word Negro to us. Way back then, they would refer to us as Blacks.

Mrs. Bethune did later use the term Negro addressing the President of the United States and white audiences, and she founded the National Council of Negro Women in 1935. It was only to "her" children that she chose to avoid the stigmatism of the term Negro.

Mrs. Bethune soon became the only real mother for me. She'd have counseling session with her girls once a week. These sessions would tell us how to carry ourselves, so that others would think better of us when they saw our carriage was "in a Godly manner."

Neither my best friend nor I could afford boarding school, so every day at school lunch time we would buy one bag of gingersnaps for a nickel and fill two glasses of water. "Will you have some caviar today?" I would ask in my most pretentious voice.

"Why, yes, with roast duckling and a spot of tea," my friend would reply. Of course, neither of us had any idea what caviar was. But the pretense kept us from feeling sorry for ourselves.

The time when Mrs. Bethune had the most influence on everybody's life was on Sunday afternoons at 3 for what became famous "community conversations." At school every Friday we'd practice all afternoon for Mother Bethune's Sunday meetings. The first bell would sound at 2 p.m. as a signal to put on our uniforms—blue skirts, white middy blouses, blue jackets, and red ties. The second bell rang at 2:30, the signal to line up, rain or shine. It seemed the whole town came out to watch us as we marched in formation to Mrs. Bethune's instructions: "The left foot's the right foot. The right foot's the wrong foot," a cadence similar to the army. We would line up in order of our size, the girls on one side, and (finally in 1923 and after) boys on the other, to march around the campus to the beat of the drum and bugle corps.

We'd march in to "Get You Ready...for the Judgment Day." Then we'd sing some patriotic airs and spirituals, put on skits and recite poems, all to applause. Then we were introduced to the important white people like the Rockefellers, the Cannons, the Gambles, and the Rhodes. They came to see the little natives shine—and we did! Every place Mrs. Bethune took us, even the most racist people would tip their hats to us, perhaps because we were dressed patriotically. In summer, we wore white linen suits to show purity of purpose.

I came to equate my own life with one of those poems
I recited: Langston Hughes' lines from "Mother to Son"
that "Life for me ain't been no crystal stair:"

> Well, son, I'll tell you:
> Life for me ain't been no crystal stair!
> It's had tacks in it,
> And splinters,
> And boards torn up,
> And places with no carpet on the floor--
> Bare!
> ...
> So, boy, don't you turn back.
> Don't you set down on the steps
> 'Cause you finds it's kinder hard.
> Don't you fall now--
> For I'se still goin', honey,
> I'se still climbin',
> And life for me ain't been no crystal stair.

(Source: *The Collected Poems of Langston Hughes*
*(*Vintage Books, 1994)

When we had performed, Mrs. Bethune got up and spoke of
those of us who had seemingly impossible longings and
suffering. Within a few minutes, she had everybody there in
tears. She'd say, "My heart bleeds for those children," and
she'd hit herself on the rear end. (The kids used to whisper,
"Mama wears her heart on her behind.") But Mrs. Bethune
was moving to the crowd. She'd cry out:

> "You say we are separate and equal, but you live
> east of the tracks, and we live west. But you use the

36

Black people to clean and take care of your children. What you haven't thought about is, if a fever breaks out on our side of the tracks, it also breaks out on yours. So it is to your benefit to help provide medical care for the poor little children. "

You could just smell the wealth of those people a block away. People would applaud. Then she'd motion boys with woven reed baskets on long sticks that would reach half-way down the aisle. The dollars would be bulging out of the baskets, and everybody would be crying.

On other days, those white women from the fancy Palmetto Club would come over and teach us how to tend gardens, cut out patterns, and make pies and cakes. Across the road from Faith Hall, we raised fruits and vegetables to sell to wealthy tourists.

One of the things Mrs. Bethune taught us was what it means to vote and how to get our parents and relatives to register. Shortly before election time one year, we were visited by a troop of Klansman on horseback,carrying fiery torches, crosses, and guns and blowing strange horns.

Mrs. Bethune ordered all the lamps extinguished. The girls sang, "Be not dismayed, whate'er betide, God will take care of you."

"We sang them right off the campus," said Mrs. Bethune, "and the next day we all voted, too!"

I'd go to Mama Mame several times a week to talk about my problems with my mean stepmother. She'd listen, then give me a pat on the back and say, "Remember, honey. That woman was your father's choice for a wife. I can't say anything positive or negative about her. But I can say to you, just try to endure. Don't forget to pray and ask God for guidance."

She called me Mac. She'd say, "Mac, you've always been wonderful. You make everyone happy. You're one of my jewels." And then she'd make me (and others) memorize gems, two of which stuck with me all my life and that I still use seventy-five years later:

1. Man's extremity is God's opportunity. When you think you have reached the extreme of your difficulty, then God has the opportunity to step in and help.

2. The darkest part of the night is just before the dawn.

I had no choice but to make A's. My brothers were content with a C or D, but I had to put myself on top. For me, A was the bottom limit. But I missed out on ways of the street, not even playing. I usually sat on the steps and watched—with a book on my lap. Maybe I thought I was better than they because I told Susie she would waste her time by playing.

When I was small, Mama Mame took us over the Halifax River to sing for John D. Rockefeller on the Ormond Beach side. We marched in wearing our uniforms and singing, "Hallelujah! There's a meeting here tonight." He talked to us. He was a nice man. So was Mrs. Rhodes, the sister of the man who founded Rhodesia, the founder of the Rhodes Fellowships.

When her girls were going out to sing, Mrs. Bethune wore a big apron with huge pockets over her dress. They'd throw dimes in her pockets as she would walk up and down the aisle. With the help of these rich people, not only were buildings built, but I can recall Mama Mame seeing that we had our tuition paid, even when Papa didn't have money.

We had two Daytona Beaches—the White one east of the railroad tracks and the Black one west of the tracks. We couldn't go to White restaurants. We could go into Ivey's, but we weren't allowed to try on any clothes.

As a result, Blacks created their own professionals. We had our own electricians, plumbers, brick masons, and policemen. It was self-help. We had to learn to help ourselves to survive.

Going across the Halifax River bridge was a big deal to us, because Black people weren't allowed on the east side of the river. Blacks couldn't go to the "World's Most Famous Beach" until Mr. Rockefeller later gave Mrs. Bethune the Bethune Beach—and that was to be a quarter of a century later. In fact, no place between New York and Miami allowed a black person to go to the beach. I used to say to my Papa, "Isn't it peculiar that the white people always refer to us as people who stink, and yet they won't let us go in God's good ocean to bathe?"

I had a terrible experience on the beach when I was still in elementary school. Since I was working as a baby sitter, "nursing" we called it, I could take little Norma Nelson to the beach because she was white. Under the walkway, I saw a white man come down and pull out his penis and begin to shake it at me. I didn't tell Mrs. Nelson when I got back home. I didn't know what masturbation was. But when it happened two more times, I told her that the man came at 10 after 2 every day. She said, "I'll send somebody down." Next day an undercover policeman came and took him away. I didn't dare tell Papa, because at $10 a week pay, I really needed that money. If I'd told Papa, he would have been down there instead of the undercover policeman—and Papa would have been arrested for being on the beach. He was a little guy, but he had a big mouth and was not afraid of anybody.

My brothers didn't get to go to school with me, since boys weren't allowed there until 1923 when the school merged with the Cookman School for Boys. I was 10 that year, and I was so happy, because I absolutely loved boys. I loved boys from the time I can remember. I was overwhelmingly carried away by boys. I had developed early, and with my large breasts and tiny waist, I was someone the boys wanted, too. If Papa hadn't threatened us with that shotgun about bringing home any babies out of wedlock, I'm sure I would have had a house full.

Nobody taught us anything about menstruation or birth control. The older black girls and women at the turpentine camp had told me how to avoid pregnancy: take nine drops of turpentine every morning for the nine days after your monthly period. If you have sex, take a douche of vinegar right afterwards. Considering that turpentine is used as paint thinner and solvent, I hate to think now what it did to our insides.

I wanted to get a boyfriend and get married. After all, my mother had her first baby when she was thirteen. But I was the unfortunate victim of enuresis (involuntary urination, resulting in bed wetting). I worried night after night about going to bed with a man and drowning him. In the mornings, I'd flip the mattress over the second I got up. I got so I could do it so fast! It sure didn't help the mattress, but it kept my secret.

Because I didn't have any shoes that fit, Missy bought me ugly brogans, a heavy dark brown ankle-high work shoe with latches on the side. She said I would wear out good shoes too fast. So I wore my Sunday shoes to school and, sure enough, they were worn out. At evening church, the rule was that children went to the front. But since I didn't have shoes, I couldn't bear to be seen in brogans. I ran all the way to New Town, several miles away, to my Uncle Charlie's house. "Aunt Jill! Aunt Jill! This is me."

"What's the matter, Tannie?"

"I can't take any more of Mrs. Ill Treatment."

Uncle Charlie said, "This is my dead sister's child. You're a good girl, Annie Mae. Jill, fix her a bed to sleep in and something to eat."

I was thirteen years old and just two weeks into the ninth grade. How painful it was to have to drop out of school. I was to study Latin: Caesar, Cicero, and Virgil. Those were the four areas. I'd just gotten into Caesar and learned that famous speech: "All Gaul is divided into three parts." I had done so well—all A's, and it hurt so bad to see my classmates getting to go to school while I was doing nothing. I yearned to go so badly.

But I'd told Aunt Jill I would not be a financial burden, so I went to a neighbor, Mrs. Thomas, who also took in laundry, and asked for a job. Her granddaughter, Julia, was my best buddy. She and I used to compete in Latin and algebra for those A grades. We both were top students. Now I would have to ask Julia what went on in school, and she tried to help me keep up.

Well, my Aunt Bay said I had to give all the money I earned to her. She told me, "I want you to go over to that old man's house, Mr. Wright, and straighten up the kitchen." When I got home, she asked me whether he had canisters out on the counter. She said she had heard Mr. Wright kept money in cans, and that I was to look for it. I refused to go back again.

So I told her brother, Uncle Charlie. He got right down on her for that. Because I refused, Aunt Bay told me I couldn't ever come back to her house. With money I earned, she had bought me pink organdy material and got a seamstress to make me a beautiful dress. But after she forbid me to go there again, she went over to Uncle Charlie's and took back my one good dress. She told Aunt Jill she would not give it back to me.

That was the last night of my childhood. At thirteen I ran off to look for a job—and the man of my dreams—make that nightmares.

42

Editor's notes:

Mrs. Bethune did use the term Negro addressing the President of the United States and white audiences, and she founded the National Council of Negro Women in 1935. It was only to "her" children that she chose to avoid the stigmatism of the term Negro.

[2]Cookman Institute at Jacksonville, Fl., the first Florida institution for the education of Negro boys, merged with the Daytona Literary and Industrial School for Training Negro Girls in 1923; thereafter, it was known as the Bethune-Cookman Collegiate Institute.

[3] Hughes, Langston. *The Poetry of the Negro*

[4] A story about that event says that the girls on campus were frightened, but that Mrs. Bethune ordered all the lamps on the campus extinguished. The girls sang, "Be not dismayed, whate'er betide, God will take care of you."

"We sang them right off the campus," said Mrs. Bethune, "and the next day we all voted, too!" (Dees 34).]

A Thirteen Year-Old 'Grown Up'

That very night I thought about Ruby Dixon, who had moved to West Palm Beach. I wrote her a letter: "Would you send me fare? I'll work to repay you." In less than two weeks, she sent me the money and a ticket, and I went to the house of Judge Curtis C. Chillingworth, a circuit court judge. I was every bit of 13 years old —but Ruby lied and told the Judge I was 17 and a great cook. Problem was, I didn't know how to cook a thing—except corn bread and fatback.

Mrs. Chillingworth was a lovely person with two children, Nina and Ann. She came in and said, "Mae, I'll let you order groceries. We're going to have fried chicken."

So I shrewdly asked her to tell me just how she liked it best, then suggested she tell me exactly how she cooked it. That's how I learned to fry a chicken, then to put it in a closed pan with butter to steam. The judge said it was the best fried chicken he'd ever eaten in his life—not knowing his wife had taught me how to cook it. That's how I did all the way through.

Another time I boiled whole, skinned beets, but they just ended up white as snow with a lot of red liquid. When I showed Ruby, she said, "Don't worry," and she ordered canned beets from the grocer and showed me how to thicken the liquid with a little flour and sugar. When we served them, I heard the judge call out, "Roz! Roz! How did Mae fix these beets? They're the best I've ever tasted in my life."

The judge was a native Floridian, born and raised right there in West Palm Beach. Since I was a Southern Black, we had sort of a strained relationship. But his wife was just lovely to me. I was the envy of almost every adult female in the community because I was getting all of $8 a week.

Mrs. Chillingworth insisted I stay in the servants' house. She said, "Don't flush the toilet at night and disturb us." Finally she got pregnant. In those days, the oldest son usually inherited the judgeship, so Judge Chillingworth announced to everybody that they were expecting a boy. But the night she went into labor in 1928 the biggest hurricane ever to hit Florida came through. So the judge went to the hospital and told me to take care of his daughters. The storm was raging and the house was shaking. No lights. No phone. We were terrified. The next day when he returned, the girls had another little sister, Rosemarie, the most adorable baby I ever saw.

The judge's mother was a typically old-school Southerner. She didn't trust any black people and constantly telling her daughter-in-law that black people would steal.

In the summer, Mrs. Chillingworth wanted me to go with her to West Plains, N.Y. That was the experience of a lifetime. Her mother had a beautiful farm in Getney Farms, where all the wealthiest people lived. I spent all of my time looking at the gorgeous antique furniture. I'd never seen anything like it. Even in the servant's room, I had a four-poster bed.

After lunch, the ladies would shop while I watched the children. Once when I was in the nursery sleeping, her father came home. Lo and behold I felt these fingers on me. He was feeling me, fingers on my breast and behind. Something told me to pick up a shoe and threaten him. "Stop! I'll tell Mrs. Montgomery and Mrs. Chillingworth on you."

He just smiled. "Go ahead. They won't believe a Nigger." I believed him. I didn't tell.

One evening when I took a walk with my new-found friend, Ida, two police officers stopped us. "Come on, baby," one of them said, taking my arm. I yanked my arm back. The other officer grabbed Ida, and within a couple of minutes they were smooching in the front seat of the police car. But my life in Florida had taught me to be afraid of white policemen. So I warned them, "I don't like policemen, and I especially don't trust white policemen. If you get out your nightstick, I'll stick you with my switchblade." (All Southern women carry them in the garters of their stockings.) The men insisted they were just being friendly, but I never went off with them. I refused ever to see Ida again.

I was walking in awe. They were just building the Empire State Building then. You should have seen me creeping along, looking up at the buildings. People had to walk around me—all those throngs of people moving fast— not like the South. Every time I saw a black face, I'd stare and think I'd see Dora, who had run away. My family said she was dead.

In fact, we knew Dora had gone up north to work for a white family. We didn't hear anything for four or five years. Then my uncle said, "Dora's coming next week and bringing a baby." Sure enough, she left Dorothy, 11 months old. I was 10 years old. My Aunt Minnie and Lula went and took the baby so we wouldn't have contact. Lula became chief cook and dishwasher. Finally Lula moved to West Palm Beach and took Minnie and little Dorothy with her.

Amazingly enough in those millions of New Yorkers, I did find Dora—though not on the street. We all went down to a shop on Second Avenue called the Chicken Shack, which had a TV, to watch the big Joe Lewis fight. When I was standing there, Rose Cohen, an old Daytona Beach acquaintance, saw me. Rose said, "I just saw Dora Clark yesterday."

Now that I knew her last name, I looked her up in the phone book and called. Dora answered the phone, but when I told her who I was, she said, "You have the wrong number." And she hung up on me.

Years later, I went directly there and climbed four flights of stairs to Apartment 11. I could hear voices inside, so I knocked. When she didn't answer, I called inside. "Dora, don't tell me you are not Dora. You are my sister."

So she opened the door. She stared at me, and the tears flowed. "You're one of my little sisters," she said. "Which one?"

"I'm Tannie."

"I never meant to forsake you," she sobbed. "How's little Dorothy? How's Papa?"

I walked in to find one child on the potty, and she introduced me to Lorenzo, then Billy and Phyllis and, unbelievably, another little Dorothy. When I got back to West Palm Beach, I wrote Dora a 15-page letter and asked Dora how on earth she could abandon her first child, then name a second daughter Dorothy. She never answered back.

I worked for the Chillingworths for a number of years. One day Mrs. Chillingworth came out while I was reading and asked, "Do you ever think of going back to school?" I said I was taking evening courses in French and Latin with Father Brown, an Episcopal priest.

"When you get ready to go, just let me know," she said.

In the meantime her children got bigger, and my sister and I went to work as pressers at a Laundromat connected to a dry cleaner. One day the boss came in and said, "Mae, all of my men have taken off. Now you'll use the dry cleaning presser." That was good pay--$25 a week. Back then dry cleaning worked on a commission, so I got a percentage increase for extra work.

Going to the job on the black people's bus—we weren't allowed on city buses in West Palm Beach—I fell hard for the cute bus driver. Odell Lambert was oh so handsome and very popular with a gift of gab so powerful he could talk a hole in your head. By this time I was fifteen years old and really had an urge to enter a sexual relationship. Since my father had warned me he'd shoot any of us who came home pregnant and unmarried, I decided getting married was the only way to go. Odell was a minister's son and called himself "Reb" (for Rebel). So instead of having his father marry us in a religious ceremony, we went over to the justice of the peace and eloped.

All too soon I discovered Odell was an alcoholic and a head hitter. He absolutely refused to go to school. He knocked out six of my front teeth, which meant I had to buy cheap false teeth. Once he struck me so hard I heard a ringing in my head for years and lost part of my hearing permanently.

In 1930, we had a little boy, William. I'd had hard labor, and the baby had to be taken with forceps. He died at 10 months old of spinal meningitis. That was another reason I was anxious to get away. Odell's family were the sweetest people in the world. Mrs. Lambert just adopted me into the family. His sister and I were close friends, but I grew to hate Odell.

My last job there could have landed me in the federal penitentiary. Brothers named Ray and Dewey Clark hired me as cook and housekeeper, but I soon found out my job was a sham. They used me as go-between in the whiskey smuggling business during Prohibition. I had a special code number to deal with Western Union packages. Men in fancy cars drove down from New York and Connecticut to pick up the whiskey the brothers brought in from the Bahamas.

Dewey, the older brother, got drunk, which was against the rules in that business. He passed out on the floor, so I took off his shoes and socks to help him sleep better. In the toe of the sock was a huge wad of hundred dollar bills. I hid it under the rug in another room. The next day he called and asked where I hid it. When I told him, he said he'd leave me one of those $100 bills under the rug, "just for being so considerate". Oh, Lord, yes, that was so much money for me! I worked four or five months for those men--until they were picked up by the feds and put into prison.

After a while, I found I was still yearning for school. I kept thinking of what my father had said: "Think of every menial job only as a means to a professional career," and I remembered his words about how I was going to become a teacher. So I called Mrs. Chillingworth and said I wanted go back to school. She said to come by, that she would give me money for school clothing.

I got on the phone to Bethune-Cookman. "Dean Bond, you probably won't remember me, but my name is Mae McClary Lambert and I want you to ask Mrs. Bethune if I could work as her maid so I could come back to high school."

"Who could forget you, Mac?" Dean Bond boomed out. "You're one of the nicest persons ever on this campus. Come on up and I'll have the package all fixed up for you."

I didn't tell Odell and risk getting my head bashed again. I just sneaked away.

The 'Sheik'
and Zora Neale Hurston

Talk about shocked. Here I'd been out since age thirteen and the start of the ninth grade. Now I was seventeen and Dean Bond classified me a senior at Bethune-Cookman Institute's first four-year graduating class. I had a year and two summers to make up for three years I'd missed—and barely a dollar to my name. But I immediately became involved in Chorale, and I was even a cheerleader.

With all these activities, I needed things I couldn't afford. I called Mrs. Chillingworth, and she said, "It will be there tomorrow." And it was. Then when I needed a sweater for cheerleading, she called Ivy's department store and told them to let me have anything I needed. I bought material and made my own dress for the prom. My big date was Wendell Tooks, who was the 'sheik' of the campus, and a volunteer preacher. His father practically owned the school. The big joke was that any time people saw us together, they'd call us "the prince and the pauper."

Wendell said he wanted to come to my parents' house. We both were living on campus. I said, "Wendell, don't. My stepmother is an alcoholic and might be drunk and embarrass me.

"Don't worry," he said. My father is an alcoholic, and I'm coming."

So I told Missy that afternoon, "My boyfriend, the Rev. Tooks, is coming. Please don't get drunk. Please promise. He's a high class person, and I don't want him to know there is a person drunk in our home." She promised. But when we got there, she was vomiting and carrying on. That was the end of bringing anybody home to meet the family.

If Papa recognized there was a problem, he never said a word against Missy. And that hurt me very much. Neither could I understand how my mother's sister, Aunt Baby, and Missy could be so close. It took me a while to realize it was because they were both alcoholics, and so was my sister Lula. Lula was also a prostitute and gambler. That meant on weekends the three spent time together cooking up moonshine. My uncle Jesse, my mother's brother, was friendly, a sweet, sweet guy. The name he called me was "Pug," because of my nose, but very affectionately. He was tight with his sister, Aunt Baby, and Lula and Missy. Right!

At Bethune-Cookman, we didn't have any spending money, but we were given jobs to work our way through school. Beginning at age twelve or thirteen, I worked my way, too. That last year in high school I did everything I could to make money. I took care of Mary McCleod-Bethune's hair and clothes. I would fix students' hair—press and curl it for a quarter. I had a part-time job doing makeup and hair at Albert Bethune's Funeral Home, but people didn't die fast enough for me to survive financially. I played for my father's junior choir which met once a week.

Mrs. Bethune taught us self-pride and self-dignity, the one thing she wanted more than anything else for her girls and boys.

That summer I was seventeen, and Mrs. Bethune got me a job as a teacher in the tiny town of Bunnell, about 35 miles north of Daytona Beach. To get students to come to my one-room schoolhouse, I had to go out into the potato fields and try to persuade the parents that their children needed education.

Since the State of Florida had no mandatory schooling for Black children—and school was offered only during three summer months, not all year, many parents considered it a luxury they couldn't afford. After all, the children were digging up potatoes, too, to help with the family income.

I gathered up the youngsters and taught them at night school. I charged them 50 cents a week. They came to my house every night. Most were boys who had to work to help support families. I couldn't stand to see them not having an education.

I especially loved working with students one-to-one. It's a selfish reason. I feel I learn from my students every day. It's reciprocal. I give to them; they give to me.

The following school year, my last at Bethune- Cookman, was especially hard. I was grieving over the death of my baby, discouraged that I'd become the victim of terrible abuse by Odell and had to leave the marriage. I was also overworked, trying to make up three years of high school in one year. Besides that, I was holding down three jobs, giving haircuts to other students for 50 cents apiece, and still not making ends meet.

In the middle of this terrible discouragement, I met my sister Lula's best friend, Zora Neale Hurston, a writer Mrs. Bethune had hired to teach drama at the college. Zora stood out—for more than one reason . For one thing, she sure didn't look like either a faculty member or student: they dressed up. She wore cotton stockings when everybody else wore silk, and she had a flat straw hat and loose-fitting gingham dress with flat-heeled shoes. Certainly the Blacks on campus looked down on her, not only because of her appearance, but because Zora hung out at the jukes, where respectable people just didn't go. Down at those noisy corner saloons, lower-class Blacks congregated around juke boxes to sneak in moonshine (because selling whiskey was illegal during the Prohibition period) and dance. When couples got juked up enough, the establishment rented bedrooms for 25 cents.

Zora had presented a musical revue *From Sun to Sun* at Rollins College, about 50 miles west of Daytona Beach. When Mrs. Bethune heard about it, she invited Hurston to establish a school of dramatic arts at Bethune-Cookman "based on pure Negro expression." Hurston later explained the reason she was at odds with Mrs. Bethune: "I found it impossible to do anything worthwhile" because there was a "student body of only 226 and the same students were needed for all the choral groups, major athletics, social groups, and various dramatic groups at the same time." (See Hemenway).

Hurston accomplished something never done by a Black before—an invitation to perform at the previously segregated Peabody Auditorium, but Mrs. Bethune wanted a pageant about the college's thirtieth anniversary—not Hurston's play. Hurston got her way—but with Mrs. Bethune's stern disapproval. By April 1934, Hurston announced she had "decided to abandon the farce of Bethune-Cookman's Drama Department."

Zora would stay with Lula in West Palm Beach when she said she went down to collect folk tales, and she and Lula used to "meet the paydays," as it was called. On Friday afternoons when men would get paid for the week, women would stand on street corners and solicit for sex. Both Zora and Lula were experts at skinning, crooked card games and playing with dice, and that's how they survived.

I had first met Zora in 1929 when I was living in West Palm Beach. Papa had tried to keep me from seeing Lula, to teach us to be ashamed of her. The rest of the family complied—all except me. I absolutely adored my big sister.

Because I was her best buddy's sister, Zora took a shine to me on campus when she arrived in January, 1934— and changed my life. She later told me that I was the only Black friend she ever had. Zora was related to us on my mother's side, and Lula, after all, was a light yellow color, like Zora and my mother. Zora's other friends were all white women.

In Daytona Beach, she lived in very close quarters with a blonde woman in a one-cabin, one-bed houseboat tied up at the Orange Street Marina on the Halifax River. The faculty and students were really hateful, always gossiping about Zora sleeping with a white woman.

I only saw her there once. After all, no Blacks had transportation, and it was a long walk from the college on Second Avenue down to the marina. Fannie Hurst used to come down and visit her—and this was at a time when Blacks and whites just did not mix socially in the South. There was talk about them, too.

Zora encouraged me to become an anthropologist. and she had much knowledge of anthropology from her studies at Barnard and her graduate work at Columbia. She conducted much of her research in the South, and I began to realize her vast knowledge of people. Thus, we had an immediate bonding of interests. I decided I would not be exactly like her, though. I would not join in immoral behavior to get information from people I studied. However, I felt my heart went out to the street people. She and I would sit on benches under the oak trees on campus and I'd pour out my dreams to her. She expressed delight and hugged me with her sweet, kind way of dealing with me.

Zora was a remarkable listener—looking at you so intensely and kindly as you talked. You wouldn't know she had all that intelligence under her belt, but you surely could feel her caring and concern. We used to say we were "on the muck" – mucky soil, uncertain ground. The Blacks denounced her as an outcast mostly because of her association with the jukes and street people, but I loved her and respected her. Even while she was teaching at Bethune-Cookman, Zora used to hire herself out as a maid and cook. She told me she wanted to "get the intimate information." While she was serving, she was listening and taking notes.

Only white people would accept Zora's unusual moral standards, but even they rejected her after she came back from the West Indies. She was really into hoo doo and the study of Zombies, and into the Yoruba religion which I later embraced so heartily. Similarly she studied voodoo in New Orleans. Her first novel *Jonah's Gourd Vine*, which came out that year (in 1934) and *Mules and Men*, which she wrote in 1934 and came out in 1935, deals with voodoo practices in the South. After the hoo doo stuff became known, she said, she felt disgraced and estranged from most people in this country. She was never accepted again in the broader cultures.

I knew dark skins had to be straight A students. Black people made sharp distinctions between light skins like Zora's and dark skin like mine. Even my own father said, "Black women sleep with their fists balled up and study evil." Because of Zora's reputation as a loose woman, Papa wanted me to stay away from her, and nobody was more strait-laced than Mrs. Bethune, who disapproved of Zora for several reasons, academic as well as moral. Zora obviously had a battle of wills with Mama Mame that couldn't be resolved during that year she taught when I was in high school.

By 1935, Mrs. Bethune was mainly interested in her own reputation and being able to get money and attention from the rich and famous. She was traveling all over the country and not so available to me during my senior year. Her daughter-in-law, who was running the bookkeeping department, didn't like me at all.

I wanted a class ring so badly, I even entered two contests, one to write "The Life and Lyrics of Mary McCleod Bethune" and another in hopes of winning prize for the rarest, the smallest or the largest book. But at the last day to apply for graduation, I still owed $27 in graduation fees. Bert Bethune's wife, Margaret, told me at 10:30 a.m. that I couldn't take the final examination without paying for it. About then, Rev. McLeod came into the room just as I was leaving. "Where are you going, Miss McClary?"

When I told him my state of affairs, he said, "I'll go back home right now and ask my wife to write you a check." I was so happy. What a narrow, narrow escape it was to graduate with no money!

Then I marched back into the meeting just in time to hear the announcements of the graduation awards. "Mrs. Annie Mae McClary Lambert—winner of the lyrics contest—has a prize of $100. And, don't sit down, there's another award for you." Rev. and Mrs. Dixon had together carried in this gigantic family Bible. I had won $50 for the biggest book! I threw it on the table. It felt as light as a two-cent piece. I still have that class ring.

At graduation, even though I had the highest grade point average--98.7 overall—another student, Neal Crosland, argued that he should be named valedictorian— even though he had a 98.5 GPA—because he had gone straight through for four years, while I had come back for a year after being gone for four and a half years and getting married, so he said I should have my grade cut down two percentage points.

"No. Her first place is right." Mother Bethune told him. "What you should know is that Mae was practically raised on this campus, almost from the time I opened the doors. Around here we go by production. Mae produced the work of most production. She earned the grades; therefore, she is the valedictorian. Mae, you are now charged with writing the class song."

I was going to Papa's house for lunch. So I sat on one of those big porch swings he made, and I wrote the song in ten or fifteen minutes. That was the happiest, happiest day of my life.

Senior Class Song Bethune-Cookman
(tune of "Sweetheart of Sigma Chi")

The years that we've spent at BCC
Are the sweetest of all our years.
And when we think of departure near
Our eyes are filled with tears.
The guidance of life we've learned from Thee,
Will help us the truth to see.

So where e're we may go
And where e're we may be
We will always love BCC

Our memories of thee will ever burn
Like the heat from the burning sun.
Our thoughts of thee will ever be
Of the good that thou hast done.
Our Love will live through the years to come
'Tho far away we be.
When We kneel to pray
In our prayers, we will say
"God bless Our Dear BCC"

When Zora left to go back to Harlem, she had urged me to come to New York. But by that time I had eyes only for my new boyfriend, Wendell Tooks. Even so, Zora and I had a very close association. I felt it necessary to protect her from all the hate and judgment.

Later, when I had graduated from Bank Street College and Adelphi University and become an anthropologist in New York, Zora frequently called me to chat. My saddest memory is the night she called me at 2 a.m., sobbing, from a jail in lower Manhattan, the Tombs, a terrible, notorious jail in New York.

"Oh, Mae, please, please help me," Zora said on the phone. She was crying and hard to understand. "I need somebody to bail me out."

I had my husband, the Rev. Wendell Tooks, get on the phone with us. "What's the matter, baby?" I asked. "Why are you crying?"

"I think I've been framed," Zora said. "Some kid who's a psycho case." And she began sobbing again. "I need $250," Zora said. "The bail is $2,500."

"Wendell will be right down," I said. So I got the money from my hiding place, and Wendell drove down to the jail and brought her back to the home of her Scribner editor, Burroughs Mitchell. The next morning she moved to an apartment in the Bronx without leaving a forwarding address. Every time I think about it, it hurts me so deeply. I was so fond of her.

According to the papers, Zora had been arrested (Sept.13, 1948) for committing an immoral act (sodomy) with a 10 year-old boy. The charge was false. Her lawyer showed copies of plane tickets and Zora's passport showing that Zora had been in Honduras for the period of which she was charged. By the time a district attorney decided Zora was innocent, nine months later, Zora wrote that she was suicidal.

I never talked to her again. She was ashamed she couldn't pay back the money, I guess, but I didn't care. I didn't want it. She was down to pauper level. She didn't have any money at all. Zora never realized any real royalties from her books. Her highest royalty was allegedly just about $700. No wonder she was a pauper! I just cared about what happened to her.

I'm sure that one thing Zora was proud of before she died was that she had the "last word" in her conflict with Mrs. Bethune which had begun in 1934. In 1956, the year after Mrs. B's death, Zora came back to Bethune Cookman to receive an honorary doctor of letters degree.

But her illustrious writing career was over. She died four years later at age 59. She was buried in Fort Pierce in a pauper's grave that went unmarked until Alice Walker, who was my son Gary's teacher at Wake Forest University, later believed she had found which grave it was, and erected a headstone. Every time I think about her this hurts me so deeply. I was so fond of her. There was a woman who would never harm anyone on purpose.

Hurston practiced a "politics of self that defied stereotypical conventions of sex and sex roles. In her personal life, she was able to embrace both masculine and feminine principles in a way that empowered her to achieve what she did. Hurston is not an anomaly, but rather part of a continuum of 'manly women' that can be traced from the United States and other parts of the African Diaspora to the African continent itself...We can also look to Zora Neale Hurston as a model of empowerment" (See Plant).

Zora had been for me in high school a role model of intelligence, caring, and courage, just as Eleanor Roosevelt would become for me in college. Too bad I had to deal with the likes of the Cahns and Mrs. Alexander Graham Bell first.

Licking the Pots
in Sorrow's Kitchen

(From an old Gullah saying, "She had lived in Sorrow's
Kitchen and licked all the pots,")

After I went one semester at Bethune-Cookman
College, Wendell and I married. Since we didn't have the
money to continue school, we both dropped out and went to
work as servants for the Cahns from 1935 to 36, and she
took us to Queens, where she had a house near Coconut
Grove. I was a personal maid, and Wendell was the butler.
This was below Wendell's dignity. "This is not what I'm
designed to do," he'd say. "I want to be a minister."

But Papa had told me, "If you have to take a menial job, do
the best you can. Remember that this is the means, not the
end. The end is a professional job." So as I scrubbed the
floor and cleaned the toilets, I was smiling to myself and
thinking, "I'm on my way to get my education."

Mr. Cahn was a Wall Street broker. Mrs. Cahn didn't trust
us. She didn't know that on my day off I took extension
classes at some college. One day she asked me to make
creamed chicken on waffles for her bridge club. She said
they raved about my cooking, but when I went into the
room with them, she called out, "You're chewing gum. Spit

that out!" I didn't confess that I wasn't chewing gum. The problem I wouldn't admit was that I had bad-fitting false teeth – the end result of Odell beating me a couple of years before.

She had persuaded Mrs. Franklin to buy the house, and she had a room there. Mr. Cahn came to us one day and said, "Wendell, Mae, I have something good on the market. I want you to invest $50 in television." He wanted to deduct that from our wages.

I heard Mrs. Cahn shout "No!" at the top of her lungs. If we'd just been allowed to make that investment, I'd have been so rich I would never have had to work again.

We stayed on with Mrs. Cahn for more than a year. On Sunday, she'd encourage me to go to Dora's, and she'd tell Wendell she had something for him to do. But one Sunday, Wendell announced we wouldn't go back to Mrs. Cahn's. "She made passes at me, and I rejected her," he said. "So she told me to just pack up and leave."

That left the burden on me to pack up all our belongings to come back to Daytona. She really did us a favor. We came back and caught the second term of Bethune-Cookman College.

Wendell wasn't much for school, so we moved down to Miami. We adopted Dora's two children: Lorenzo (we called Larry) was born in 1938 and Billy in 1941. I had several miscarriages, but never had another child born to me after my baby William died.

In January of 1936, we took servant jobs at the home of Colonel Montgomery in Miami. The Montgomerys lived way, way out near Mrs. Alexander Graham Bell, their best friend. One reason they liked me as cook was that Mrs. Bell said I made the best fried chicken or biscuits she'd ever eaten. But when I'd go into the room, the snooty Mrs. Bell wouldn't even make eye contact, let alone speak to me.

Mrs. Nell Montgomery was a new wife. According to my best friend, Celeste, who also worked for her, Nell's aunt had been the Colonel's bookkeeper. So Nell made a point to go along with her aunt and please him—and keep her promise she'd marry a rich man. Nell Montgomery was nice to us, but the Colonel wouldn't condescend to talk to Blacks about anything.

His long-time white chauffeur, Walter, hated him— and vice versa. Walter would say, "I'm going to fix the S.O.B. I'm going to leave him stranded on Fifth Avenue in New York in all that awful traffic." To help get even, Walter bought duplicate groceries to distribute to poor Blacks. I had to make doubles of everything, just so he could get even. One day the Colonel bawled Walter out, and he came out crying: "Now I'm not only going to buy duplicates, but I'll deliver the goods myself."

Walter said he'd overheard the Colonel tell Mrs. Bell and some others that I was the best cook he ever had. Walter's advice to me was: "Tell them you and Wendell have found two wealthy spinsters with more money than the Montgomerys have and that you have agreed to go butler and cook for them." They couldn't stand to think anybody in the country was wealthier than they were. For example, he bought the second tallest palm in the world. (They already had the third tallest.)

So the next morning I did it exactly the way Walter told us. I told Mrs. Montgomery I had some sad news. I said she already knew that I was taking extension courses in history from FAMC (Florida Agricultural and Mechanical College), and that now I would have courses on Thursday as well as Saturday. I told her that the sisters would let me have both days off, not just Saturday as I had now. I made up an exaggerated salary we'd receive.

"We can do better than that," Mrs. Montgomery said. "I'll talk to the Colonel and remind him that you don't spend as much as the other cooks we had." (This was even after Walter was tripling the grocery order to give food to the poor!) When she came down on Tuesday morning, she told me she and the Colonel had decided to take a cruise and let their friends stay at the house. "We already told them you are an excellent cook," Mrs. Montgomery said. "We're prepared to offer you more than the sisters have." And they did.

The worst thing about working for the Montgomerys was their house manager, Mrs. Jordan. She'd go out and cut fresh flowers all day long to put in different rooms of their house. Every time she'd cut through the kitchen to give me advice: "The Colonel thinks this....the Colonel says that..."

Finally, I told her: If you come in here and interfere one more time, I'm going to kick your ass."

She told Mrs. Montgomery, who called me in and said Mrs. Jordan was afraid of me. I suggested Mrs. Montgomery not only tell Mrs. J just to take care of her own business, but that she insist Mrs. J return the space heater of ours which she'd taken. She did, and from that day forward, Mrs. Jordan detoured the kitchen.

While the Montgomerys were in New York, Walter kept his promise. He took the Colonel to Fifth Avenue during Rush Hour and never returned to the car. Meanwhile, I played the horses with my new salary. I played for a whole year, and even had my own bookie.

With my winnings, I opened Mae's Beauty Shoppe. It was a classy place with four operators. Wendell was the shampoo man. I had a hunch about a horse named Meadow Lark and told a girlfriend who lived up the street to put $20 on him to win, then so much for second and third place. A little while later she called and said, "Come quick! I don't care if your hair is in curlers!" I ran up there to find she'd doubled the bet. So I got $80 to every $1 I'd bet, a big, big hit.

The day the Mongomerys returned, she came into the shop and called out, "Mae, Mae!"

I answered, "Over here, Nell."

"What did you call me?" Mrs. Montgomery was indignant and walked off.

"Since you addressed me in my own business by my first name, I'm addressing you the same way," I said.

She came back the next day. "I told the Colonel about your shop. I'll pay you double what you earn to have you cook for Mrs. Alexander Graham Bell. She and I are having the Club of 100 over, and she insists that you're the cook."

I knew that snooty club was all WASPS (White Anglo Saxon Protestants). So I told her, "Go down to the employment agency. I'm sure they'll have a Swedish cook."

I did very well owning my own business. I worked hard. I had white customers, too. Jewish customers wanted to come on Sunday when the shop was closed and Wendell was at church. Sometimes I had as many as three or four Jewish customers. They'd pay me double.

I can't remember a time since I was thirteen that I couldn't put my hands on a dollar. My father always told me, "When you're away from me, save money for a ticket home or an emergency."

The biggest "emergency" of my life happened one day in 1940 when I was away from the shop, waiting for my sister, Susie, to come down on the bus to visit me. Wendell had just got out of the shower. Suddenly I felt as if an electric shock burned my skin.

"Why did you hit me?" I asked Wendell.

"Girl, I didn't touch you."

"What time is it?"

"10 minutes before 7," he said.

"I would have sworn you hit me with a wet towel."

Wendell answered the phone call which came from the beauty shop. He said, "The police just phoned the shop. They've accidentally shot your sister."

"What! When?"

"She got caught in the line of fire on the bus when the police were shooting at a suspect. She was just waiting in a crowd for the bus. The guy ducked behind her. It happened at 10 to 7," Wendell said. "Mae, that's the exact time you said I hit you with a wet towel."

I called Bessie back and asked her to divide up my clients with the other operators. When I got to the hospital, Susie was alert. "Tannie, they called to ask you to give blood?"

We went in. It's most unusual to find two sisters with Type B blood. Then they gave us a hearty steak and told me she was in surgery. The doctors said she could be okay. But, meanwhile, I sent Wendell to call Papa. Albert Bethune, who ran a funeral parlor in Daytona Beach, drove him down.

He said, "Brother McClary, I think you'd better say your prayers. She doesn't look too good to me." Tuesday morning when we walked into the hospital we smelled a pungent odor.

"That's not me you smell," Papa said. I went home. At 20 minutes to 2 I sat up in bed and heard a strange sound: "Yrang, Yrang."

I visualized people in chariots singing as they floated up to the sky. I lay in bed wide awake and just waited. Then I heard the doorbell and looked at the clock. "Go see who it is," I told Wendell.

He came back and read slowly the message from Western Union. "It says Susie Arthe passed at 20 minutes to 2 this morning." Like our mother, Susie was exactly 27 years, three months and 12 days old when she died.

I had no heart for doing anything, including the shop, after that. I was desolate. Susie and I had been so close that everything else kind of lost its meaning.

Later, a man Judge Chillingworth had sent to prison got revenge when he was paroled: he killed Mrs. Chillingworth and Nina and dumped their bodies in the river. I felt as if I'd lost another mother. She had been so good to me.

When I started having a lot of back pain and my thumb was hurting, I went to Dr. Johnson. He told me: "You know something? The human body is like an old car. You can keep patching it up and it will wear out completely. I suggest you go back to your shop and put it up for sale." And so I did.

The next day I called up Dean Bond and announced, "I'm coming back to school. I'll arrive sometime Sunday."

"What do you mean you're going back to school?" Wendell asked.

"Just what I said. I'm leaving tomorrow."

I left him there to run the shop and went right back to Mildred's house, picked up my little boys, and headed off to college –and to war.

Editor's Notes:

From an old Gullah saying, "She had lived in Sorrow's Kitchen and licked all the pots," quoted in Hemenway 323.

My Mentor --Eleanor Roosevelt

When I came back for college, I was the hair dresser for Mama Mame every morning. When the President's wife, Eleanor Roosevelt, came down to stay, which she did frequently, I fixed her hair, too. I was living on campus, but I went every morning and helped those two women dress properly. I made sure that the dresses were pressed and they had matching shoes.

Eleanor Roosevelt was a honey of a person. She always wore her hair in a bun. As I did her hair, I'd pat her on the cheek and give her a kiss. She'd tell me, "Mae, you're a very unusual woman. And your research is brilliant."

Mrs. Roosevelt talked to me about a meeting with her husband and Churchill. So I did research on the Dunbarton Oaks conference, the prelude to the League of Nations. I was the chief researcher to explain to the students at BCC what lay in back of this meeting and what were the goals and objectives, that sort of thing. That's why she thought I was such a brilliant, nice person. It has never been in my mind to make a distinction between people. I don't know why.

Every Friday I lectured for the students, and she attended. That's how I became increasingly interested in the League of Nations. I was the chief researcher for all big events that happened. Mrs. Roosevelt was so supportive and encouraging to me. I really wanted to be like her—a lover of people. She could smile so easily, and I really admired that. She never seemed to see a distinction in people by race. She did whatever I did, helped in the garden, baked pies, or whatever, right beside us.

She took our Glee Club to Hyde Park to sing for the President and his mother. He asked each one of us our names and shook our hands. His hands were so strong, even though he was in a wheelchair. He had a marvelous way with people, and even his mother, the dominating matriarch, was receptive to us—not at all snooty like Mrs. Alexander Graham Bell.

I admired Eleanor Roosevelt and Mrs. Bethune, who served as my mothers, more than anyone in the world—they were my idols. The influence Mrs. Roosevelt had on my life was because of her relationship with Mrs. Bethune and because of the way she treated the students. She was so friendly, giving a kiss or a hug when she met someone. She, like Mrs. Bethune, was the kind of person I wanted to be all the time. I loved them both equally--with a passion. I believe I loved them most for their personalities, for the way they loved people. The way I love people is still what I like most about myself, and I could see myself through the behaviors of these two women.

At BCC during the war we couldn't help but feel we were directly involved in helping to change the world for Black Americans, not only because of all the time Eleanor Roosevelt spent on campus, but because of Mama Mame's far-reaching activities.

After the President died, Mrs. Roosevelt lived across the street from the Little Red Schoolhouse, where I taught on the Avenues of the Americas. She'd frequently come to the park and bring her little Scottish terrier, Fala. While the children played, I'd sit on the bench and talk with her. She took time for every single one of those kids—as a way of doing something special for me. If one of the children came up while I was talking, Eleanor would say, "Excuse me," and take time for that child. They loved it. They couldn't wait to get to that park to talk to Mrs. Roosevelt. Just the idea of playing with the dog and talking with the wife of the (late) President of the United States was so appealing to those kids. Lord, was she a beautiful person! She wasn't beautiful by our physical standards, but she had the soul of an angel.

Back then Mrs. Bethune was known to be one of the few women in the world who had talked back to the President of the United States. But he appointed her Director of the National Youth Association during the War and she traveled throughout the United States.

I was hired as director of the Daytona Beach USO, a city-wide unit. The problem was that my second job there was to teach pool –and I'd never played even one game. So I went to the library and read a book, then memorized it so I could teach. By the time the war was over, I could shoot with the best of them. Meanwhile I knit cardigan sweaters by the dozen for the Red Cross to send overseas.

Recently a television special used an old newsreel that showed the same room at Hyde Park where we sang for the President. It also showed Eleanor coming into the room at Warm Springs where her husband had died, and there sat a woman beside him, his mistress. In the film, Eleanor went over to her husband and kissed the body and said, "Franklin, the children and I are going to miss you." Then she walked out of the room and began pacing the floor. As I watched the film, I cried and cried, remembering being in their home with them, remembering her overwhelming tenderness and support for me, knowing her pain. What a great woman!

After FDR died, she brought his monogrammed silver-handled cane down for Mama Mame. I don't think Mama Mame ever again walked without it. It was her proudest possession.

Another time the two women were riding in a railroad car when the conductor asked Mrs. Bethune to sit in the "colored section." Without a word, Mrs. Roosevelt walked right back there with her. That must have blown the conductor's mind. I wouldn't trade my experiences with those two women for anything in the world.

At first I was living at Bethune-Cookman without my husband. Finally a man paid me $3,000 cash for the shop. It was wonderful. For the first time, I didn't have to beg or borrow groceries or rent. I paid cash. Then Wendell moved up. His father had a store in Daytona, and Wendell agreed to work for him.

Wendell's parents were very fine. We didn't have to buy food. I rented a house with six bedrooms on Lincoln Street for a very small amount of money. Besides, there was a big farm at Bethune-Cookman, so faculty and students could get all the fresh vegetables we wanted. We spent very, very little for food.

Wendell was doing practically nothing. He took a couple of classes at college, which I paid for. He took—not earned—most of the money which came into the store during his hours and spent ALL the money on his own clothes. I supported him and the children and me.

I finished all four years of my college work in two terms and two summers. I studied day and night. I was determined to be that A student. I made A's in every class except one: Human Development and the Family. I talked back to Miss Cray when she told us that "In marriage, women are nothing but garbage receptacles for men to dump sperm into." She flunked me for that.

Even so I ended up placing first in the very first four-year college class of Bethune-Cookman College. As I walked out of the ceremonies in my cap and gown, clutching my diploma, my father stood in the lobby with tears of joy streaming down his cheeks. He was so proud of me. Just then Mother Bethune pulled me out of line, said for me to wait for the end, and then told both Papa and me to go into her office.

"I have three telegrams offering teaching jobs for you, Mae," she said. "But you're not going to take any of them."

"Why not, Mama Mame?"

"I want your first job to be right here on the faculty of Bethune-Cookman College, to be able to say this was your first professional job." A few days later I signed a contract.

Mae with her beloved
father James McClary

Mae at her eighth grade
graduation from Bethune
Cookman school

Turpentine Camp company store.
Photo courtesy of Debra West.

Mae receives an honorary doctorate from The
Bank Street College in New York

Mae and her fellow students all lined up behind Mrs. Mary McLeod Bethune for her famous Sunday matinees.

Dr. Mae Walker as Director of the first African-American Studies Program at SUNY Stony Brook

Dr. Annie Mae Walker, resplendent in African-style attire, shows her husband, Bill, one of the items given to her Thursday night.

Dr. Mae Walker, with husband Bill, at an awards ceremony honoring her with a lifetime achievement award by the NAACP.

Dr. Walker with husband Bill Walker

President Lyndon Johnson asked Mae to create the model for the first Head Start Program

Dr. Mae Walker organized after-school classes as program chairman of the Central Long Island Branch of the NAACP.

After-School School

Arithmetic holds the attention of Paris Stanford under the tutelage of Mrs. William Walker of Amityville, who's also on the Plainview f a c u l t y. Mrs. Walker organized the Amityville after-school classes as program chairman of the Central Long Island Branch of the National Association for the Advancement of Colored People. Eighty-seven pupils are tutored Monday through Friday from 3:15 to 6:30 p.m. in the special classes.

Mae worked for the "uppity "Mrs. Alexander Graham Bell.

Marilyn Monroe and husband Arthur Miller invited Mae and Bill to a dinner Marilyn cooked

~Eleanor Roosevelt~
"No One Can Make You Feel Inferior Without Your Consent."
www.InspirationBoost.com

Mrs. Roosevelt mentored and encouraged Mae, who looked up to her as a person of great virtue and respect.

Mae served as captain on Dr. Martin Luther King Jr's famous marches through Alabama.

Malcolm X lived in Mae's home while his mosque was being built

**Mae and Maya Angelou were room mates as
Danforth Scholars at Yale University**

**Zora Neale Hurston persuaded Mae to become
an anthropologist like her.**

**Mae called her friend Ella Fitzgerald
"Miss Ticket, a Tasket"**

**Mrs McLeod Bethune mothered Mae all
during her childhood and was Mae's idol.**

Mae's poem "Blackness, Like a River" was inspired by the St. John's River at Lemon Bluff near the turpentine camp. Photo by Michele Boudreau Hawkins

President Lyndon Baines Johnson asked Mae to pioneer a new program called Head Start.

The Black Scam for Teachers

From 7 to 8 in the morning, I taught a BCC college class in psychology. From 8:30 to 2, I was the fourth grade teacher. After that I went back and taught another college class in Methods and Materials in Elementary Education from 3 to 4 p.m.

My total salary of $710 for the 10-month school year wasn't enough to cover our living expenses, so I took on two additional jobs. Dr. Bethune's son, Albert, ran a funeral home. I did hair and make-up for the viewings. On rare occasions, I played hymns for a service. The problem again was people didn't die fast enough for me to earn a living. Over the weekend, I worked in Edith Johnson's beauty parlor next to the Bethune campus.

While I was at the college, I became involved in the National Association of Colored Persons (NAACP). A classmate at BCC and close friend of mine, Harry T. Moore, asked me to be Co-Petitioner of the Black Teachers Association. Of course, there was also a White Teachers Association we worked with, since every benefit we were able to scrounge helped them even more than us. Harry and

I sued the State Department of Education in Florida to get equal pay for black teachers.

The pay scale for all teachers, black and white, was allegedly based on education: A grade for a Master's Degree plus 30 hours, B for an MA, and C for a bachelor's degree. But no black teacher could qualify for A or B. Only one black person in Florida had a Ph.D., Ray Gray, 30, the president of Florida Agricultural and Mechanical College, the state school for Blacks.

I discovered the whole system was a sham. Whites were automatically graded A or B, Blacks were all C. Within those B and C categories were levels. As a black person, my salary was much lower than the C categories for white teachers. Even with a Master's degree, Harry was still rated C; therefore, in 1944, we took the Equal Pay for Equal Training case to court.

If anybody back when I was a teenager had told me that I would one day be sitting in a predominately white school teaching white students, I'd have told them they were liars. You had to go to Bethune-Cookman or Live Oak or FAMU (it was FAMC at that time). The first black person who challenged the system came from Bethune Cookman, receiving his bachelor's degree there. He wanted to go into the master's program at the University of Florida. They turned him down, of course. The court decided the state must pay for any black person who wanted to get master's degree and doctorate degree outside the state, but the student wouldn't accept that. He insisted on equalization within the Florida state university system.

With these test cases, the KKK got very interested. They frequently rode horseback down Second Avenue, their torches illuminating the white sheets over their heads. Both Harry's family and mine found burning crosses on out front lawns and death threats on our doors: "Stop now—or die." Months later the words would be carried out with a fatal fire bomb.

Meanwhile, Dr. Agnes Snyder and Mr. Trayer of the Bank Street College in New York were sent down to BCC with a team to evaluate our Lab School for accreditation. The school was funded by BCC and Volusia County, so the county sent an evaluator to make sure we taught the county program.

The problem was that textbooks for black children, published in Atlanta, were totally different from those bought in New York for white children in Volusia County. For example, the Social Studies text I was supposed to teach said the world was divided into three zones: torrid, temperate, and frigid. The example for torrid (like Florida) was an African child named Lem Weeche sitting naked in a banana tree, eating a watermelon. I was horrified at having to give such a biased view that would hurt our children's self image. So I changed Lem to Bill and we laughed at the publisher's ignorance—until the children looked out the window and saw Mr. Saunders, the evaluator, approaching. Teachers were supposed to follow the text book exactly – and not supposed to include "frivolities" like art and music. We timed it so that just as he'd reach the classroom door, I'd say: "Children, time to put away the clay activities and get out our textbooks." When he entered the room, I'd say, "Children, what page are we reading?" They'd answer aloud, in unison, "Page 43, Mrs. Tooks." While Mr. Saunders was present, they even remembered to use the name "Lem Weeche."

Dr. Snyder sat in the back of the room, tears running down her cheeks, barely able to keep from laughing out loud. After one of these sessions, she said: "Mae, you're not only a gifted teacher, but a fine actress. I've arranged for you to get a full fellowship at the Bank Street College." (I learned later that she dipped out of her own pockets to do it.)

When the telegram announcing the scholarship came, I went to Mother Bethune for advice, explaining my husband was out of town, working for the Red Cross during World War II, and I didn't know how to answer those people. I was afraid he wouldn't approve of going to New York.

I thought she and I could make the decision. After all she had given a famous speech that said, "The true worth of a race must be measured by the character of its womanhood. . .she exerts a unifying influence this is the miracle of the century.("A Century of Progress of Negro Women" was delivered to the Chicago Women's Federation). Mama Mame said, "You need to stretch. Now you've grown beyond Bethune-Cookman College, but I can never tell you to go against your husband's wishes. Why don't you ask your father?"

"I'm not going to make a decision that affects your husband," Papa said. "Go talk to Wendell's dad and ask him to represent his son."

So I went down to the store and asked Father Tooks. He said, "Don't wait for that sorry son of mine to come back.

Just go and tell Mrs. Bethune that you will go now. Do you want me to call her?" I nodded, so he called Mrs. Bethune for me and said he was making the decision for his son, that Wendell wasn't doing anything with his life, and there was no reason I shouldn't go onto higher heights. Mrs. B was happy about that.

"Since his father made the decision, I feel better." Mama Mame said. "So you go with my blessings." Then she maneuvered so I could go to Bank Street with all expenses paid. She'd fallen in love with Dr. Snyder when she was down here, too.

I never got a letter from Mrs. Bethune after I left there. She wouldn't take the time to write to someone so insignificant as I. You'll find letters she wrote were to Roosevelt and other big time people. Mrs. Bethune, off the record, had become a very snooty, ego-inflated woman who lived and thrived off all the accolades she got from white people. As a matter of fact, she made choices and distinctions between darker and lighter skin people. We used to say she was high yeller oriented, but all of Albert's wives were high yellers. The last one, Margaret, turned out to be an alcoholic.

I loved her and respected her, but I knew her shortcomings. And I knew that to reach the heights I had reached, I had to be an A student, being a dark-skinned person. In those days, even in Alpha Kappa Alpha, of which I became a member only because of my scholarship — even then Black people made a distinction between light and dark-skinned people. Now my sister Lula could get into anything, and she was well accepted by everybody around— not only because she was considered pretty, but because she was a high yellow.

It wasn't hard to leave Bethune. I'd gone to Columbia University Teacher's College the summer before that, and was beginning to get a peek into progressivism and progressive higher education. Soon after I graduated from Bethune-Cookman, I was accepted at Columbia and went there the first summer to start work for my master's degree in early childhood education. But this Banks Street scholarship came up that next school year, so I let Columbia go.

And so it was that I was in New York on that Christmas night in 1944 when the KKK bombed Harry's house in Daytona, killing him instantly. I knew they'd be looking for me, too.

Bombs and Bank Street

That day Harry's wife also died of injuries. About six weeks later, I came home to East Elmhurst in Queens about six. I'd just gone down to the basement to stoke the coal furnace, then raced up to the second floor bathroom. Halfway down the steps, I heard this God-awful blast. I knew: the KKK had found where I lived and bombed me, too.

I was terrified. I didn't know whether to run back upstairs or down and out of the house. Knees shaking, I decided to go down to the basement since the sound seemed to come from there. But nothing was wrong in the basement Then I went to the kitchen and saw glass shards all over the floor, the big window shattered, and something dark and big on the floor. I ran, gasping for breath, next door to the Helm's house, which was semi-attached to ours. She and her husband were German. "Mrs. Helm, Mrs. Helm!" I cried out. "Somebody has thrown a bomb through my kitchen window."

I called Tony, who is Italian and a policeman, who lived two doors down. We'd just started talking when Mr. Helm came in through the back door. "I was listening to you," Mr. Helm said. "Nobody would do something like this but a damned Dago!"

"Swallow those words!" Tony grabbed him by his collars, lifting Mr. Helm's feet off the floor. "Mae, did you hear anything after the bomb blast?"

"Yes, I heard footsteps heading this way," I said. "But that was after I'd already gone down to the basement to check on the problem, then run out the door."

"That proves Mr. Helm is the bomber," Tony said. "I'll lock the S.O.B. up. You be at court tomorrow to press charges."

When the time came, I didn't press charges. After all, Mrs. Helm was a very nice person and had let me in when I was in trouble." I found out there had been only one other Black family try to move to East Elmhurst. They'd been tortured and sold their house immediately. I wasn't about to move.

I'd been through torture myself—just to have the privilege of becoming a teacher in New York. In September, I failed the state's oral exam for teachers. My grammar was perfect, but they said I had a problem with dental d's and t's. I pronounced route so it sounded like the word "r-out" and Houston with a long u sound, not like "house," which is how New Yorkers pronounce it. So I hired a private speech tutor, who immediately recognized that I came from a background of Seminole and African-American. He also discovered I was tongue-tied, so I went through surgery to free the frenum. It was so painful. I had the stitches in over the fourth of July holiday. Then they discovered they hadn't cut back far enough, and I had to have more surgery. But before school started the next September, I had my teaching certificate.

I loved being in New York as part of Bank Street College. I had the advantage of having two teachers from Columbia at Bank Street. I had Roma Gans, whom I'd had two courses with at Columbia, and I had another teacher, a very famous psychology teacher, Dr. Benzer. Her book is *Let Me Be As I Grow*. She was warning teachers and mothers,

> Don't try to change the lives of these kids according to your knowledge. Take their ideas and put them first and guide them and direct them along lines they wish to take.

Also Lillian Smith taught me at Bank Street, a white woman from Georgia, the author of *Strange Fruits* and *Killers of the Dream.*

Everything useful I know I learned at Bank Street. For example, I know about what happens with stomach acid from absorbing too much citrus. I eat about six every night. But let it hurt, let it hurt. I love my oranges every day. I learned there why California oranges have thick skins. The climate is conducive, but not the moisture. The soil is too dry, semi desert, even with irrigation. All the things that are obvious in the social order I learned at Bank Street.

Right from the start I was considered a social outcast at the college, and not only because I was the first black student. All those other girls from Sarah Lawrence and Radcliffe and other Ivy League schools went to lunch together. I remember one of them coming up to me and said, "What the Hell you got to smile about anyway? You're always grinning." I was hurt and embarrassed.

Soon I became friends with Polly, who was a Tobacco Roader from West Virginia, another one of Dr. Snyder's scholarship winners. She was a good-looking blonde girl. I was living in West Harlem, she in East Harlem. Later Catherine Cook, one of the "black bourgeoisie," but very learned, came to be my close friend. We even got closer at the Little Red Schoolhouse. Bank Street operated on the premise of looking at the whole child and with the idea that school life is living, not the preparation for living. We all studied John Dewey's ideas.

He placed an emphasis on the whole child—social, emotional and psychological. He said school was not preparation for life, but life itself, and I adopted his theories wholeheartedly.

For our student internship, Polly and I taught with Lewis Garland. He looked at Polly the first thing and asked if she were married. When she said no, he replied, "You will be married." He wrote a book and said he loved her.

I bossed Polly around to a place to get bridal material, and I told her, "You're going to marry in blue." She had no choice. I made the wedding gown. We met in Virginia, right across the bridge from Washington, D.C. I was the matron of honor. She stayed with us. (Today she still sends me a Christmas poem.)

For our graduate thesis, four of us did a major project. Clarice Pentock was from Vassar College, Sue Rockland from Sarah Lawrence College and also rich.

At first appearance, they came off snobbish. But it had just been what sociologists call "consciousness of kind." When it came down to working together, they were wonderful, generous people. We studied the transformation of Harlem, looking at his change from the affluent apartments of the exclusive rich to the war-time occupancy by Puerto Ricans and Blacks from the South.

I was always interested in the topic on which Lucy Sprague Mitchell founded Bank Street, and that was on the relationship of man and the earth. Man was a part of environment; man was in position to make choice of changing the environment or leaving it as it stood. A definite relationship.

I came from two different philosophies in my own life. The Seminole Indians did everything to preserve the environment. The Blacks were part of the industrial movement to change environment to further society. I was always curious to know my father's and my mother's backgrounds. With respect to my father, especially, the distortions are just numerous. With respect to my mother, there are no true recordings about what happened.

In my book about the Nunn family history, I wrote: "Just like a tree planted by the water, we shall not be moved," the words from an African-American spiritual of the 1830s. The prologue says what I really believe as an anthropologist: "The past is a measure of the present/ And the assurance of the future./Neglect the past and a man/ Becomes an embarrassed fugitive,/ Without a yesterday or a tomorrow." I added:

History is the study of man/woman's past achievements, frustrations, hopes, and longings. In this context, historic knowledge of an individual's genetic lineage is essentially important because it provides a mirror, reflecting the self-image, and, therefore, self-identity. To know one's family history is to know oneself; that is, to know that the foundation for personality formation was laid in the institution, family. Indeed it is within the context of family that the individual develops his/her concepts of self, values, and worth in relation to others in the world. Consequently, the lack of knowledge of one's family history suggests that there is a likelihood of an individual's becoming "an embarrassed fugitive without a yesterday or tomorrow."

.

While I was at Bank Street, my hated stepmother, Missy, died in August, 1946. I had my first teaching job and had just earned $510 for six weeks work when Papa called to tell me my step-mother had died, and the undertaker wouldn't bury her. He said the charge was $500. I'd just got my very first pay check, so I sent it to Papa through Western Union—which charged me $10 to send it.

I told Papa to tell people I had an emergency and couldn't get to the funeral, and for him not tell anybody I sent him the money. The truth was, of course, that I didn't have any money left to come myself.

At Bank Street, you get to know yourself, and to feel good about yourself. In the South, a coal miner's family is characterized as different and bad. The turpentine workers were the lowest rank of all. At home, the combination of Melissa and poverty had made me feel miserable. But at Bank Street you felt like a queen. It was like Teachers College at Columbia. Everybody, from children to teachers, was called by first name. I was known as "Mae, teacher of eights." So I went from teaching black children to an all-white classroom. They always gave me rapid learners. The sky was the limit because the State of New York considered them important.

I'd never heard of focusing on the whole person— the psychological, the potential for intellect and physical development. I learned that the best educators can do is look at the components and work within a framework.

While I was at Bank Street, Dr. Snyder said, "A husband and wife should be together, so I'm going to find a job for Wendell and appeal to him to come up." She sent him fare and got him a job working for the post office. That was the first job Wendell ever had. Since she knew he was on the lazy, sophisticated side, she arranged for him to ride with the Special Delivery guy, only he would have to get out of the mail truck to take the mail to the door.

Wendell said it was too cold, even after she bought him long johns. So she got him working in the Post Office annex to load mail into burlap bags. Then he complained he was allergic to the dust from burlap; it upset his allergies. Dr. Snyder was still tolerant. So she got him a job sorting mail inside. He had to learn a scheme for doing this.

In the meantime, he kept insisting he had to be connected with a church and needed a congregation. He was studying theology at Union College, and I was paying for it. I'd finished Bank Street by that time. Once he quit the post office and joined a church, but it was not the kind I attended.

I attended Abysinnia Baptist Church. Adam Clayton Powell was my minister. He had just divorced his first wife and married his second wife, Hazel Scott, a very famous pianist from someplace in the West Indies. His first wife was a black movie star named Frieda Washington. Hazel had a son named Adam Clayton Powell III. (After Hazel, he married a Puerto Rican girl, who also had another boy, ACP IV.) Lord, could that girl play the piano! I don't know anybody in the world who could play like that all over the piano. She played jazz and blues. Wendell didn't like it because Powell had married what Wendell called "that woman of the world," and the church wasn't a Southern Baptist where they clown and carry on. Once he joined that association, they sort of convinced him that I was not on his level.

Aside from being lazy and not doing anything, Wendell became extremely verbally abusive. Our marriage became even more estranged, though we'd had problems since the early 1940s. When World War II started, I was afraid he was going to be drafted, despite his poor vision, so I urged him to go to the Baptist convention and ask for ordination. He did. By stating he would like to work in depressed areas, they deferred him from the draft. But I don't think there was a single choir member he didn't sleep with—or altar boys either! Yes sir! When he preached on those hot Sundays in Florida, I'd have to send his suits to the cleaners on Monday morning. Invariably there was a note in the pocket saying, "My darling, I'll meet you at such and such a motel Monday."

I confronted him, and he'd deny it. So I'd call my sister Susie, the one who admitted she loved to fight. She'd come down from Daytona, to Miami, where Wendell and I were living, and I'd point out the choir member who'd written the note. Susie would find some way of luring her to a dark place, and would beat her up. She'd say, "Tannie, you can take this stuff, but I can't! You're too good to Wendell for his own good."

By the time we got to New York, Wendell cursed like a drunken sailor. His church convinced him I was not on his level. I said if he didn't mend his ways and stop cussing and yelling and criticizing, I would leave him. We were renting then. He said he'd try to work on it. But I used to go downtown Manhattan around sixth street where they had tennis courts, and I played every weekend. I was quite good, too.

One weekend I teamed up with a young woman, whose problems seemed like mine, so we sat down and talked about it. But she said, "I'm going through psychiatric help to see if I can stay with my husband." She recommended Dr. Brown, a black psychiatrist over at NYU.

I went to see Dr. Brown at NYU on Sunday instead of going to church. He let me talk, talk, talk that whole hour. He said, "It seems to me like Wendell doesn't need help. He's satisfied with his life. But you've moved into another vein now; you've become more enlightened. You have abandoned many of the Southern traditional ways and come up here where you don't see yourself as a Negro, but you do see yourself as a person. You need to make your own commitment because Wendell isn't about to change. Unless you can accept this analysis I've given you today, I can't use you as a patient. Otherwise you wouldn't subscribe to anything I would say to you."

I was so mad at him for saying I was the one with the problem. I dropped him like a hot potato.

About four or five years later, I was still teaching at the Brooklyn Community School, my first job out of Bank Street, where I taught seven years. Oh, I miss those little ones now, I tell you. I loved teaching little children. Third grade was my absolute favorite. I'd see them like little birds with their mouths open, on the threshold between babyhood and childhood. In one gulp, they want to take in all the knowledge of the world.

My friends there were Carl, who was Black, who dated another teacher, Gertie, a white from a German Jewish family. We all went to Greenwich Village together, which is where Wendell and I left them. The next morning Charles Aaron Price, Jr., one of my third graders who was the newspaper publisher's son, came in waving a copy of PM (*Progressive Magazine*). "Mae, look at the paper! Carl's beaten and Gertie roughed up. Now they just beat him because he's a Negro."

Paul Lockman, a doctor's son, socked him in the mouth.

"Mae's a Negro," Charles said.

"She is not!" Paul socked him again.

At this point, I stepped in and told all the children the history of the word Negro, which comes from the Latin word *niger*, meaning black. "In anthropology, this pertains to a major ethnic division of the human species whose members are characterized by brown to black pigmentation." After I explained why I fit that category and gave them acceptable synonyms for the word, they calmed down.

One day while I was teaching there in 1953, I got a call from Rose Thayer, whose husband, Nathan, was a plastic surgeon. She was once described as "that heavyset blonde woman who stands on the corner preaching Communism." She had three little blonde girls. She told me I needed to adopt a baby whose father was black and mother was also a German Jew. The parents weren't married, and neither family would accept the mixed race baby.

By the way, I never use the term illegitimate, because I believe there is nothing either legitimate or illegitimate about intercourse. Let's just say "Out of wedlock," though in today's society, we don't need to say anything. So few children will live with both parents by the time they reach elementary school. We also need to recognize that there are no pure races any more. We're all of mixed genetic heritage.

Three days later I went down to the Jewish agency and came home with Gary. Rose Thayer would even come over to Queens on winter break to baby-sit him. For Christmas, she bought him a chinchilla suit, as well as clothes for every phase of the baby's development.

That baby had everything—except a real father. Wendell abandoned us for his new "true love" –a young man, also a preacher.

Editor's Notes:

Portrait of the John and Sarah Jane Nunn Family: Roots-Ghana, West Africa. Daytona Beach, FL: Wesley Bros., 1983.

[2] Words from an African-American Spiritual, USA, 1830s.

[3] "Prologue" in _Portrait of the John and Sarah Jane Nunn Family Tree: Roots-Ghana, West Africa, North Carolina, USA. 1.

[4] Morris 889.

Marilyn Monroe and 'the Shrink'

I took little Gary to school with me — and sometimes took my problems with my students home with us. In one case, I had to speak harshly to a parent about the "framework" at the child's home. Mary Miller had come to me at school one morning all dressed in Black and sobbing. "Mae, I feel my life has ended," she cried. "Arthur wants a divorce, though he says we'll wait until after Christmas to separate."

"What's the problem?" I asked.

"He is engaged to Marilyn Monroe."

Every few days for several weeks, she came and got me out of class to talk about her problems. Then Bobby Miller, who was in my eights [third grade] class, bragged at Show and Tell time that he'd gone to his father's apartment and Marilyn Monroe had let him drink two beers.

I was furious with Arthur—even though I'd really liked him until now. I'd known him for several years. In fact, his daughter Janie had been in my class three years before. He was a very quiet, soft-spoken guy. Just talking with him, you'd never know he was such a genius when he wrote. Arthur was wonderful helping us to raise money for the school by putting on *Death of a Salesman* as a benefit performance for Bank Street one year, and *The Crucible* the next. It seemed so senseless for him to leave the wife who'd helped him through college to go off now and marry some movie star. I told another teacher, "I could choke him. I could kill him for dumping the mother of his two children."

Right after the Show and Tell incident, I was furious. I called him up and told him I needed to talk with him immediately. "I'll come by and drive you home after school," he offered. "We can talk on the way." When he pulled up, Marilyn Monroe was with him. She asked if there was a butcher in my neighborhood. When I said yes, she told Arthur to stop, that she would cook supper while he and I talked.

We all walked into the butcher shop, and little Gary—who was about four at the time—announced, "Mr. Tony, can you get some steaks for Marilyn Monroe?" We heard the clank of knives and everybody in the shop rushed out to get a glimpse of her. I took little Gary aside and explained he had no right to go around dropping names like that.

Marilyn was a good cook, though Gary couldn't eat a bite just for looking at her. I couldn't believe she could have an effect like that on a four year-old. She was such a sweet gal, smiling and chatty, very outgoing and lovely. She'd call to check up on how Bobby was doing at school. I never knew the degree of her disturbance until I read about it after she had divorced Arthur. Arthur was so quiet himself. He let both women he married do the talking for him. Mary and Marilyn were both glib talkers.

The Millers weren't the only ones having problems. The school where I was teaching was mostly Jewish, except for Jim and me and Eleanor Foster, the director. They were all dealing with psycho-analysis. So I went into her office and I told Eleanor, "I still have problems with Wendell. I can't make up my mind whether to quit my marriage to Wendell. I feel guilty every time I think about leaving him"

She had a heavy, deep voice when she said, "My darling, you need psychological help." When I told her I couldn't pay for it, $50 an hour, she said, "Mae, I'm going to lend you the money for one year if you will take psycho-analysis. Then you can pay me back a little at a time."

I went out to lunch with the rest of the women faculty. Only Jim was non-Jew and non-female. We had a warm corned beef sandwich on rye, and an hour later I had god-awful cramps. The Black woman who cleaned our building said, "It appears to me you have an ulcer." I didn't even know what it was. Instead of going home, I took the bus straight to Dr. Alter, our family doctor (I taught two of his children at school) who put me on Mylanta or something like that and ordered some hospital tests for a GI series. When he looked at the results from the GI series, he was so upset.

He was just pacing up and down the floor, up and down. He said, "Wait a minute. I'm calling Miriam. I want her to come over here and console me." So his wife came over. "It's not usual that I share something about my patients, but I want you to come over as quick as you can to console me. Mae has a bad duodenal ulcer," he told her, "and I'm so upset." So Miriam comes and puts an arm around me.

I finally said to him, "I have this. You don't have it, Dr. Alter. I'm the one who should be comforted, not you." His wife cracked up with laughter.

He said, "I think something is bothering you, Mae, and you need psychiatric help. Dr. Schulach is right upstairs and I'm going to make an appointment for you."

So I went to see Dr. Schulach. I thought, I'm not going to get on that darn couch. I'm going to show him that he's sick and not me. I told him all about how mean Wendell and Melissa were. After a while, about ten minutes before the end of the session, the doctor said, "Mae, you are in big trouble with yourself. Wendell and Melissa are fine. They're very contented with who they are and where they are. You are your own worst enemy. You're the one who needs help."

I burst into tears. "I think you're being very unfair and mean to me," I told him.

"Do you want to quit before you get started?" I said I guessed not because somebody was lending the money, so I kept with it. For a whole year though, I refused to lie down on his couch. I had to go through downtown through Brooklyn. The lights were on, they were singing carols, and it was so beautiful – so beautiful to the normal person that is. The more I saw and heard of Christmas in store windows or street corners, the angrier I got. I thought, "I feel miserable. I don't see what there is to celebrate."

When I got to Dr. Schulach's office, he said cheerily, "Hi, Mae. How are you?"

112

"I'm not good," I said. "I don't know why all these people engage in all this commercial activity. I denounced everything connected to Christmas.

"I can't help you there," he said. "People are going to do what they want to do."

"Excuse me, but I have to go to the bathroom," I said.

The more I talked, the more often I had to go to the bathroom. I left the session five times. Then Dr. Schulach said, "Stop making excuses to avoid your feelings. You go to the bathroom and piss for the last time and make it final. Quit trying to escape."

When I got back into the room, I said, "Dr. Schulach, help me get on the couch." And he did. He sat on the couch beside me and patted me while I wept.

He said, "I'm so glad this has finally come to a head. Tell me how you feel."

"When I came here, I felt a heavy burden from head to toes. You know, I think I'm at a point where I want to forgive Melissa. Now the load has dissipated and I now have pain just from the neck down," I told him. "Now I can see our resentment for each other was mutual, and I disliked her from the moment she walked in my father's house. Now I understand why she resented me and, beyond that, brutalized me. I was woman of the house, and she had taken my place."

When I left that session I felt so good that I went into A & S and bought new draperies. I'd quit Wendell and I got my very first Christmas tree of my whole life. Before then, I wouldn't celebrate Christmas or Easter ever before, not even with the children. But this time I called up Celeste Boyd, my best friend (now dead). "Guess what! I'm going to have a Christmas party for close friends." I even bought a new couch for the living room.

She came over to the party and bought Cecil Battle, a guy I fell for like a ton of bricks. I'd invited 40 or 50 people. We only had a record player, but I danced for the first time in my life. Neither Papa nor Wendell ever approved of dancing, so there was never dancing. Also for the first time I tried a strong drink, a Manhattan. It hit me like a dagger through my heart. But it was the best time I ever had in my whole life. And I discovered I loved dancing. Pretty soon I got dizzy and vomited. I vowed never to get drunk again.

Shortly after that, about February or March, I walked into Dr. Schulach's office, and said, "Guess what. My head cleared all the way to the top."

"You don't need me any more."

"No, I am cured."

You know he was a very good guy, except those times right at first when he yelled at me, "You sure are in trouble."
I was still going with Cecil. He asked me to marry him. I got scared, so I called Wendell and asked him to come back to New York. I wasn't so sure of Cecil. First of all he was handsome. Oh, Lord, what a handsome man! His brother was a movie actor and he could have been, too. He said, "I'm sort of glad you asked Wendell to come back, because I know I was rushing you and trying to force you into a position."

Oh, I was a devil. I thought I was master of my own fate. We had been promised a two-family house. The upstairs family, Harry and Liz taught with me in Brooklyn. When it came time to move in downstairs, the landlady took one look at Wendell and me and said, "Oh, I made a mistake. I promised this house to somebody else."

I looked at her, and said, "Well, we don't have laws against discrimination," I told her. "But I promise you I know why this has happened. Since Harry and Liz recommended us and they are White, you assumed we would be White, too. Since we're not, you won't rent to us."

When that happened, I told Wendell I was going to buy a house. "What in the hell do you mean? We don't have money to buy a house." But I told him I would get it from somewhere. So I went to see my Grand-Uncle John Byrd, who was in real estate. I told him that night I had $255 in the bank. You realize you can't buy a house for that. My uncle advised me to make a list of 100 people who could loan me $100 each, because he had a house for $10,500 that was just beautiful on East Elmhurst, out near Flushing. My uncle told me that the man could have sold it long ago, but he's waiting to meet the right people. Isn't that something?

That night I was at a party for the Brooklyn Community School and came across Jack Kurtz. He told another parent, "See that woman. She's the greatest woman in the world. Anybody who could do what she's done for my son, Richard, is unbelievable. I'd do anything in the world for her." The other man said the same thing about what I'd do for their children. They called me over there, and Kurtz said, "Mae, come over here. What is it that I can do for you?"

Well, here was my moment. "If you'd do anything," I said, "You can lend me money for a down-payment on a house."

"Are you serious?"

I said yes. Kurtz said he wouldn't lend me money, but he'd do something better: he'd take me and introduce me to his banker. One of his chain of three furniture stores was across the street from Manufacturers-Hanover Bank. Jack Kurtz made an appointment after school and he personally took me over. The bank was closed, but the bank president let us in. Kurtz told him he wanted the bank to give me a loan. I needed $1,500, 10 per cent of the loan, plus $500, to get the $2,000 down.

"Now, Mr. Kurtz, you know I can't do that. She doesn't have collateral. I can't give her a loan."

"Yes, she does," said Mr. Kurtz. "You're looking at it. She has me, and I have three furniture stores and I do all my banking with Manufacturers-Hanover. "

The bank president went down all the reasons he couldn't loan me the money, that I didn't have a car or a big savings account and a lot of other reasons.

Kurtz pushed his chair back and said, "Come on, Mae." He started out.

"No," the bank president said.

"Kiss my ass," Kurtz answered, and we started toward the door.

The bank president stepped in front of it, and said, "No, I'll let her have the money." Ordinarily it takes three days to process a loan. That guy gave me the check within five minutes.

Jack Kurtz was a short man, verbose, really dominating. He dominated his wife, his children, his employees, everybody. He compensated for that smallness just the same way that Herbert Hoover of the FBI did, by bullying people. Then Kurtz suggested I go over the Savings and Loan to get the other $250. Since I already had the money from the bank, the S & L also gave me a check the same day.

So I went over that afternoon to my uncle and announced, "I didn't have to go to the other 99 people on my list." So I got my house on East Elmhurst in Queens.

After the closing, Uncle John said we'd celebrate with coffee and buns. When we got there, he said he wanted to introduce the neighbors to us, and he came back with Mr. and Mrs. Helm. What I didn't know was that Blacks had been refused houses until then. We were the test couple.

When I saw Mr. Helm's face, I thought that man would fall dead any minute. John said, "There's a customer. That's why I gave him my card."

Sure enough, that was the introduction. This was a Black man engaged in gerrymandering, and he was an expert. Within a few weeks, the Helms called and said their house was for sale. Shortly after that, East Elmhurst was a predominately Black community.

But Wendell said he didn't want any house. He wanted to go back to Florida "where people have sense, and because New Yorkers don't have the God in them."

Bill Walker and Ella Fitzgerald

"You was easy to get," Bill said.

"Absolutely not! I played hard to get."

"Nope! You was easy. I know. I was there. I was the greatest!"

The morning I met Bill I'd been to a singles party the night before. I'd been writing to Arty Worth, a professor in Philadelphia, a very stiff guy. When I got to the party, three other women "pen pals" were waiting for him, too! Obviously he didn't show. I was telling Cousin Mildred, "I'm gonna write that son of a gun right now and tell him how mad I am!" I was on page two and really getting into the anger when the doorbell rang.

I opened the door for our friend Charles Jones, and this guy with him yells, "Hey! It's cold out here! Can I get in?" Then he walked right in past me. He followed Charles to the pantry and came out with a beer and a complaint. "This beer isn't cold Can I get some ice?" I'd never heard of such a thing. I told Mildred this guy was a presumptuous son of a gun and arrogant. Charles introduced Bill as the chauffeur for Ella Fitzgerald.   He wanted to show off his voice.

Charles went over to the piano and played "Trees" while Bill sang the words. I nudged Mildred and said, "This guy's good."

But Bill kept his eyes on me, wanting me to make a comment to him. We applauded, then Bill did "Sometimes I Feel Like a Motherless Child." For the last song, he looked at me and belted out, "I Love You, Truly" as if he meant it for me.

"How about that?" Bill asked.

"That's singing all right," I answered.

Then he sat between Mildred and me on the sofa. "Can I have your phone number?"

"Indeed you cannot!" I replied.

"I want to call you."

"No. I don't even know you."

"Where's your bathroom?" he asked.

I told him it was upstairs. Then I heard him walk from the bathroom area into my bedroom. "What's that lousy son of a gun doing?" I asked Charles.

"Getting your number off the telephone."

When he came down, Bill said he might as well go. "I'm not getting anywhere here." I think Charles had told him about me. As they were leaving, Bill announced, "I'll be back around two tomorrow to see you."

"I'm busy," I answered. So about noon, I took Gary, who was two, and went to see my girlfriend, Marie. I purposely stayed there until after supper. When I came home about 7 p.m. to put the baby to bed, do you know Bill was still sitting on my front steps!

"I thought I had avoided you, Buster."

"No, you haven't avoided me. And you can't—ever! Go upstairs and put the baby to bed."

So I invited Bill in, only to find Mildred moaning. She was in labor. "I'll take her to the hospital," he said. About 4 a.m., the phone rang. "Congratulations! We have a little girl!" He told me he'd gone out and bought cigars. I couldn't believe it. I'd met him the day before, and here he was, posing as the baby's father.

About 7 in the morning, I heard the doorbell ring. I looked over the banister and there was Bill Walker with two armloads of groceries. "Open the door. I'm going to fix you breakfast," Bill announced. And sure enough, Bill made two eggs each for himself and little Gary and me.

"Daddy, can I have one with a hole in the middle?" Gary asked.

"No baby under three in my house is going to have three eggs for breakfast!" I announced. Bill calmly went ahead and made Gary a sunny-side up third egg.

After that, every time Gary saw him, he'd call "Daddy, daddy!" Even when I took him to the barber shop, he asked, "Barber (Mr. Duncan), do you know my daddy? He's a big old pretty man with a hole in the top of his head," he said (referring to Bill's bald spot)."

But still Paul Williams would call me in the morning, and they would have words about me. I told Bill, "You and Paul can fight it out." Paul would usually meet me at the bus stop, so Bill said, "This morning I'm walking you to the bus stop."

The two met each other halfway there and started laughing at each other. "That's all right. You were there first," Bill said. "But I'll make you a bet. I'll marry her."

"OK," Paul said. "You've won."

Cecil continued to call me for years after that---until Bill came over to phone and said, "Cecil, this is the last time you are going to call my house. Mae said you two are just friends, but I don't like this kind of friendship." Cecil didn't call again.

I told Bill that Arty was coming to spend the weekend with me. "Oh, that's fine," Bill said. And he went out and bought steaks and wine and champagne, all sorts of stuff. He said he was buying it for Arty. Well, Arty came up Saturday, but Bill had spent the night with me Friday night. (Oh, Lordy, I know they're going to take this book out of the school!)

Meanwhile, Arty came to see me Saturday and found Bill's pipe upstairs in my bedroom. "Well, I see Ella Fitzgerald left her pipe here," he said. The thing is that every time Bill had come by, he'd left a note saying, "Ella was here." That stinking Arty had been reading those notes.

"I don't like it," Arty said. He was snobbish and owned a lot of property. He said he wanted to support me so I didn't have to work. One night when Bill came over, I was writing a letter. I told him it was to Arty, telling him I didn't have any intention of giving up my life career, and that I was with Bill. I finally told Arty it was impossible to sham and fool each other any more. "I've decided Bill Walker is my steady guy."

Before Bill and I were together, Gary had been fond of my ex-husband, Wendell. But now Gary refused to go over there or to identify ever again as his father. He even tore Wendell's picture out of my photo album. "That man's picture doesn't belong," he said.

I was teaching then at the Little Red Schoolhouse and lived on East Elmhurst in Queens. Bill saw me as I was leaving with Little Gary on the bus.

"Just leave him with me instead of waking him up like this," Bill offered. I said yes. While I was gone, he kept the kitchen floor spotless and had a meal waiting for me. He told me to let the cleaning lady go. Well, here he was doing everything, all the cooking, all the cleaning, and fathering Gary.

By that time I realized I didn't have too much choice. Bill had brought his clothing over to the house little by little until he had a closet full. My baby called him "Daddy." How could I not marry the man?

We went to Alexandria, Virginia, to get married one weekend. The minister was ready, Bill had the rings, and I forgot the blood test results. The minister told us to go to the Department of Health and get another test. So we did.

In those early years, Bill turned out to be both feisty and a womanizer—and, yes, quite a liar about those experiences. He'd come up the steps and I'd chase him back down, using my high heels in my hands as weapons. I'd raise my voice loud in sin, but Bill would never talk back in anger. I was the hell raiser.

"Now, Mae, calm down," he'd say. "We don't want little Gary hearing us angry." Or he'd say, "This loud voice is beneath your dignity."

Then he went through a time where he'd down a fifth of booze every weekend and run up my credit card bills at the liquor stores. I threw all of his clothes out the window three times, and once lifted a heavy purple recliner, his favorite chair, and set in and all his clothes in the driveway.

Finally I sent him down to the mortgage holder, made him relinquish his claim to the title of both houses we owned, and told him it was sobriety through A.A. or divorce.

After a few A.A. meetings and time in a treatment center, Bill recovered. I went to Alanon to learn how to cope better. Bill thanked me over and over for forcing him to deal with alcoholism and save our credit records—as well as our marriage. He never drank again.

For many years, he drove Ella Fitzgerald around by day and worked as a ticket agent for Trans World Airlines in the evenings Ella wasn't performing. Fame hadn't gone to her head. She stayed casual and down-to-earth in most things. But even though they became close friends, the two always addressed each other as Mrs. Fitzgerald and Mr. Walker. She'd call me and sweetly ask my permission to talk to my husband about performance dates and would bring him back fancy shirts and gold jewelry from trips abroad.

Bill and I spent a lot of time at her house the week Ella's sister died. I went in the kitchen and found the singer stuffing several huge pieces of chocolate cake in her mouth. "Now, dear, don't eat all that fattening cake to deal with sad feelings," I advised her. "You're fat enough already."

"But I love it, and right now I don't care," Ella told me— and went on eating more cake.

When she left with her aunt, Virginia Williams, who'd raised her, to go to California, Bill took a job driving truckloads of storm windows and doors. His territory extended all the way up into New England.

Finally when Gary was just about two years, not quite, just being toilet trained, and my niece, Lois, was staying with Papa because he'd had a stroke, she called me up in New York and asked me if I would come because she wanted to go to high school and needed some help. So I said, "Let me call Lula." So I called her and asked, "If I send you the money, can you help for three weeks before school is out? The baby is just being toilet trained, and we still have outdoor facilities at that house."

That was prior to 1958. He'd lived two years in that condition. (Feb. 15, 1958, he died.) The screens were all torn from the house, and mosquitoes were very bad. Her answer was, "That's your damn daddy, so you come yourself. I'm not coming." That was the cruelest thing that could have happened to me. I was teaching and had three weeks left in my semester, too. Bill offered to not work and stay home to take care of Gary. I went to Florida and got things taken care of.

When I married Bill, we were still living on East Elmhurst in Queens. There he got hooked up with a guy to cut records of his singing. He was going to go pro. But Bill was not out-going then, sort of shy actually. He referred to my taste as long-haired music, and he was uncomfortable with educated people. Gradually this changed.

With Bill, it was kind of like, "I'll make myself a man." Until he met me, Bill had been more of a street person with the values of street people. He often said, "I'm not at ease around your 'educated' friends."

Born in Richmond, Kentucky, near Cincinnati, Ohio, Bill was always responsible for taking care of his younger brother and sister, cooking the evening meal, and cleaning the house while his mother worked. His brother, Joel, would ignore his mother's direction and go fishing. Bill would do all the chores, never even tattling on his brother.

After high school, he worked in a foundry, then enlisted in World War II, where he served in Italy. He was back working in the Cincinnati foundry when Ella Fitzgerald came into town for a concert. By the time that evening was over, Bill had been hired as her New York chauffeur.

I'd met her the night she made her very first amateur appearance at the Apollo Theater in 1935, singing "A Tisket, A Tasket, a green and yellow basket. . ." Every time I saw her after that, I'd call out, "Hello, Miss Tisket a Tasket." She'd just grin. Even though Bill had an agent and cut a couple of promotional records, he never even told Ella Fitzgerald he could sing.

I investigated his educational benefits through the GI Bill. I also managed to get him a full scholarship to the School of Social Welfare at SUNY. Sure enough, they paid Bill's tuition and he went on to finish his master's degree in social welfare. He went from high school to getting a M.S.W. in just three years by working six days a week. I helped him with his studies by assigning my graduate students to do research for his thesis, and I typed the thesis.

Meanwhile, he went on to take two more courses with me. Bill graduated with in 1976, and immediately got a job working at Central Islip Hospital, then Pilgrim State Hospital. His job was to place hospital patients into half-way houses in private homes. He also had to prepare them to live in a home after spending years in a state mental institution.

Soon after our marriage, Bill asked, "Why not live in a suburban area like Long Island?" That was at Midnight on a Saturday night. Early Sunday morning we drove out to Amityville. There were two model homes, and naturally I wanted the most expensive model, The Oakcrest, for $38,000. When Bill said we couldn't afford anything like that, the salesman, Mr. Archer, told us that the builder, Mr. Pratter, was excellent and that the homes were well worth the money.

"I know a Mr. Pratter," I said. "Does he have a daughter, Susan?"

"This woman knows everybody in the whole world," Bill said.

But Susan wasn't easy to forget. When I was teaching the eights at the Little Red Schoolhouse years before, the children were all stacked up at the door. All of a sudden one child screamed bloody murder and gave a push and all the 32 others fell down against me, knocking me down. There I was on the bottom. I asked my student teacher, "What happened, Gail?

She said, "Susan backed up, and everybody fell down. Are you hurt?"

"No, I'm not hurt," I said, "but I want you all to go ahead. I'm going to have a talk with Susan."

She was screaming bloody murder, "Please, Mae, please don't punish me!"

I surprised her. I said, "Sit down in my lap." I put my arms around her, and I said, "Susan, you've been very angry with the children in our class. And yet you complain to me you don't have any friends. You have to act like a friend to have one."

"Mae, I won't be mean any more." So we worked out a way for her to help others and stop screaming.

The next day she asked her mother, Violet, to have me to dinner. It was a long way from my house. I lived all the way over on East Elmhurst and they lived in downtown

Manhattan. I got there early, and Marcie hadn't gotten home from his law practice. I said, Violet, where's Susan?

"I made her go up in her room," Violet said. "She was bad."

"She was bad, and she was the one who invited me to dinner? Give me my coat. I'm not staying here. I'm not having dinner with you. I came to have dinner with Susan."

Violet started crying. She said, "Mae, I thought I was doing the right thing by depriving her from seeing you." Susan was taking all this in from the top of the stairs.

She cried, "Stay, Mae. I'll be good from now on." I made them both promise not to tell Marcie so we wouldn't spoil a good dinner and my visit. We didn't. But from then on at school, we saw a different, happier child.

I didn't hear any more about that incident until Susan was in the eighth grade. She was in Mrs. Seikman's class, and I had taught her daughter in third grade. Mrs. Seikman called me and woke me up in the middle of the night. "Mae, may I read something to you? I asked my students to write about the most important experience in their whole life. And guess what Susan talked about? The time she pushed the children down and you held her in your lap and told her what it meant to be a friend. And, Mae, she is some writer! She wrote, 'Mae is a teacher I'll always love as long as I live. She taught me a lesson I'll never, never forget."

And that's the last time I heard about Susan until Marcie Pratter called Violet and I went out to lunch with her. Susan had just decided to drop out of college in Boston and wouldn't discuss it with her parents. So I went over, Susan came down, and within an hour decided to go back to college.

The next day the salesman called us. "You are the luckiest woman in the world," he told me. Not only is Mr. Pratter giving you the Oakcrest you like, the bigger house for the price of the little one, but he's throwing in $17,000 worth of extras. I've never seen this in my whole life."

Since I was teaching in Massapequa, I used to drive by every day to check on it. It seemed so slow going. "Mr. Pratter is awfully fussy with this house," the worker told me. "He said everything has to be the best. Only the best people are allowed to work on it, and that's why it's so slow." And, sure enough, it was one of the most beautifully constructed houses ever in the world. He turned the garage area into a paneled den. He suggested an extra closet, and a breakfast room in line with that 11 x 17 kitchen with stools for snack bar, and two and a half baths, a half extra. The address was 76 Glen-Malure Street in Amityville.

In 1963 I was teaching fourth grade at Southridge Elementary. I decided to start the Freedom School, an after-school program for children who were failing in school and had not been promoted, partly as a result of something that happened in my dining room at home. I kept calling Gary for supper, then finally found him using a brush and soap to scrub his face. At dinner, I asked him why he would do that. "I have to wash the Black off," Gary told me. "My teacher doesn't like me because of the color of my skin. I'm going to tell my daddy to come to talk to her."

It was time yet again to change some White teacher's racist views.

Editor's Note:

Overheard conversation between Mae & Bill Dec. 4, 1995, three weeks before his death.

Marching with the King

Selma, Alabama, March 25, 1965. We have marched four days with Martin Luther King, Jr., thousands of us, at least as many Whites as Blacks, walking the highways and streets—thousands of KKK and other racists on foot, horseback, and in cars, sneering police, crowds throwing rotten fruit and invectives. Yet we sing and believe, "We Shall Overcome."

King has shown us how to fall to avoid injury to our head and vital organs when state troopers and local police brutalize us. Hundreds have been arrested and jailed, but thankfully I have escaped so far. Of course, we have our own bondsmen along. I wear my African finery. "Aunt Jemimah" is the kindest of the ugly names hurled at me. "Yankees go home" read picket signs in the hands of shouting, ugly racists. They are especially abusive to the White marchers among us, at least as many as Blacks.

"We are still in for a season of suffering," King preached from the steps of the state capitol in nearby Montgomery this morning. He urged Blacks to have the courage to register to vote. "We must keep going," he said.

But I am afraid. Exactly one month ago Jimmy Lee Jackson was shot and killed by a state trooper near here. Two weeks ago demonstrators attempting to march from Selma to Montgomery were brutalized by state troopers. Last week the Reverend James Reed from Boston was beaten to death on a Selma Street. And this has followed a summer where three workers were kidnapped and killed and their bodies buried, thirty-seven Black churches have been burned, thirty homes bombed, eighty civil rights workers beaten, and more than 1,000 arrested.

Directly in front of my car is one driven by a lovely, lovely woman, Mrs. Viola Liuzzo, a White mother of five children from Michigan. She is transporting marchers. A Black man sits in the front seat; another Black man is in the back seat. Suddenly we are surrounded by the White-robed KKK. Two of them grab the man in the front seat. I see them shoot him. On the other side, Klansman shout "Nigger Lover" to Mrs. Luizzo. She is shot three times in the head, blood spurting everywhere. Even I can tell she is dead. Afraid, I crouch on the seat, my head on my lap, police whistles, shouts, sirens. I expect the KKK to hit us next.

If they know who I am, I am a sure target, for I have been a leader in the movement for five years now. I am called "Ma" by university faculty and students and the civil rights followers. It is a title of respect, not a nickname, I have earned from my young friends, Jesse Jackson and Stokley Carmichael, from my minister, Adam Clayton Powell, and from leaders of the Southern Christian Leadership Conference.

Every Sunday night we in the NAACP meet in the Black and sometimes White churches of New York and New Jersey to have a pep rally and plan the Monday sit-ins, lie-ins, and marches of the Black Liberation Struggle. I am an organizer and spokesperson. My role is to fire them up. We start every meeting singing "We Shall Overcome," then a spiritual like, "Just like a tree planted by the water, we will not be moved." Then I speak about how Blacks deserve equal education, equal jobs, equal pay, equal opportunity. I ask them to take a pledge to show up for Monday's demonstration, and then we sing "We Shall Overcome" again.

Once a dozen of us went to a grocery store that discriminated against Blacks. We all filled shopping carts to the brim, then put them in a circle, blocking all the checkout counters and walked out, abandoning the carts. When the World Fair came to Flushing, hundreds of us parked our cars on the Long Island Expressway, then we lay down in the middle of the pavement.

Martin Luther King taught us leaders the art of passive resistance. He reminded me of the example of Gandhi. You'll remember that even though he was of the highest caste himself, he chose to sit in the lotus position, wearing only a loincloth, in the middle of the untouchables, until he brought about social change. Dr. King was very cordial, but what I was most impressed with was his powerful intellect. After my son Gary shook his hand, he didn't want to wash his own hand for a week.

Passive wasn't Bill's nature where I was involved. On one of the first marches in Amityville, some men standing in the back of a pickup truck hurled insults and names at me.

Bill broke ranks and started after those guys, but one of the trainers grabbed him, and said, "No, Mr. Walker. Don't react." After that, Bill wasn't allowed to march.

"Good riddance!" Bill told them. "I won't sit around while anybody insults my wife. Besides, I've been thrown out of better places than this."

As an administrator at the university, director of Black Studies, I could easily work my schedule to join the Monday demonstrations and make several speeches a week all over New York, New Jersey, Connecticut, and Philadelphia on the subject of "Blackness and its Responsibility."

For the first time since FDR, we had a President who believed in civil rights.

Editor's Note: "On June 11, 1963, President Kennedy delivered his strongest civil rights message ever. "We face...a moral crisis," he said. "A great change is at hand, and our task, our obligation, is to make that revolution...peaceful and constructive for all." Only days later, Kennedy sent a comprehensive civil rights bill to Congress."

Chills still run down my spine when I think about our march on Washington. We had taken the Freedom Train from New York. There were 250,000 Blacks and Whites, priests and rabbis, rich and poor folk gathered in front of the Lincoln Memorial to hear Dr. King. All of a sudden we saw Jack and Jacqueline Kennedy pushing a baby stroller with John John and holding Caroline by the hand. You couldn't see any secret service men about. I'll tell you, baby, such cheers went up from the people. We were so happy, so very happy!

It was a glorious experience—though not without its hardships. Washington was closed up tight—no place to get anything to eat or drink, no restrooms. I think businesses were terrified of us. Luckily some of us brought along sandwiches and thermos bottles. In the middle of that huge throng, I lost Bill and Gary. I called out for them and started looking frantically, but everybody was singing, "We Shall Not Be Moved." You could hear the echoes and chanting off all the buses down in the square. Finally somebody from New York recognized me and told me Bill and Gary were sleeping in the grass nearby. I was so relieved.

King's speech ended:

When we allow freedom to ring, when we let it ring from every village and every hamlet, from every state and city, we will be able to speed up that day when all of God's children—Black men and White men, Jews and Gentiles, Catholics and Protestants—will be able to join hands and sing in the words of the old Negro spiritual, 'Free at last, free at last; thank God Almighty, we are free at last!'

As everyone knows, just two weeks later four Sunday school students at a Birmingham, Alabama, church were killed by a bomb explosion and President Kennedy was assassinated two months later. But all the violence prompted Congress to pass the 1964 Civil Rights Act.

In the 60s, we still had token Blacks in universities. For example, SUNY had more than 25,000 students, but just 68 of them were Blacks. One of the amusing things that came out of the movement was that students demanded—and got —co-ed dorms. As a result of this "shacking," we ended up with a shocking number of babies. Then students successfully demanded child-care for babies while they were in classes. It was not my place to condemn students for their activities,

As a member of the faculty Senate, I sponsored two students activist groups: Students for a Democratic Society and Black Students United. When SDS decided to boycott classes, the administration took a counter move. The President announced: "Any of you teachers who are thinking of being supportive and not crossing the picket lines, just remember that students have to pass final exams or they won't graduate."

I went to bed fretting over the problem of how I could avoid crossing that line, but yet assure that my students got what they needed for life—that college diploma. By morning, I'd figured out what to do. I called the reliable leaders and had a secret meeting.

"You will arrange that every student comes alone to my house to take the exam," I warned them. "If any one of you rat on me, here's what I'll do. I'll bring you before the administration and I'll point a convincing finger at you and tell them you are dangerous and should be expelled. Now you work out the schedule to get everybody here one at a time."

So every single student showed up at a different hour until I had handfuls of those little blue books with the essay exams. I bypassed the picket lines and took those books in to be read by a committee. And every single student passed —because nobody squealed!

Editor's note:

Bullard, Sara (ed). Free At Last: A History of the Civil Rights Movement and Those Who Died in the Struggle." Montgomery, Ala.: Southern Poverty Law Center, nd, 30.

[2]Ibid. The Council of Federated Organizations campaign created "Freedom Summer" to bring attention to voting abuses; "a thousand college students, most of them white, were brought to Mississippi to register voters and teach in Freedom Schools. If the white volunteers were beaten or arrested for voting activities, civil rights leaders reasoned, the country might take notice" (29).

[3] Ibid. 24.

[4] From King's famous "I Have a Dream" speech that day.

Freedom School
and a Run for the Board

I realized we had to do something to change the perception of teachers toward Black children. I talked with the local chapter of the NAACP and several churches and civic groups to sponsor a free remedial tutoring program for the children of Amityville. Two weeks before the start of the school year, I put an ad in the paper for volunteer teachers. Immediately 22 teachers responded. Each teacher agreed to give a minimum of two hours a week free of charge. Two churches gave us space, and I went around to bakeries to give us doughnuts and cookies.

The Jewish students tutored on Saturday. They'd take children to play tennis or go ice skating. We developed a wonderful mentor "pals." Two Black sororities, Alpha Kappa Alpha and Delta Delta Delta and the Alpha men all pitched in.

It was one hundred per cent successful. Not one child who attended our school failed to pass the next year. More and more children from all walks of life, all ethnic groups, and nearby communities came. I worked my head off. And that's also how I happened to get my second master's degree at Adelphi University. For each teacher I supervised, I got three credits. We had testers come in and the results proved our school worked.

The NAACP adopted the program nationally because we had such tremendous success. By the third year in Amityville, the state of New York took over the schools and the funding, deciding this program was a necessity. It was the tenor of the times, and I stepped right into it.

In April of 1964, a number of political causes asked me to run for the school board. I didn't want to. I was teaching, I had a small child, and I was working on my doctorate degree at Columbia. Besides, there was no chance a Black woman could win. But they convinced me to run, the first Black woman to do so ever, just so our platform could be heard. The Central Long Island Branch NAACP Bulletin reported in their April issue:

> In announcing her decision to run, Mrs. Walker, a veteran of more than 20 years experience in education, and a six-year resident of the district, said that 'since the strength of our democracy resides in the preparation of our children for citizenship,' her campaign will be 'dedicated to the cause of high quality education for all our children.'

Pretty soon I began to get calls to speak before civic groups, and it was obvious that I insulted people just by running. At one of the meetings, the Knights of Phythias, a fraternal organization, I could see faces grimacing and others shaking their heads as I spoke. Here's what I said:

De facto Segregation is Amityville

The issue of de facto segregation in the Northeast School is the most pressing of the several problems that confront our school district today. This unresolved and mis-handled problem is serious impeding the educational progress of many of our White and Negro students. It has also had an unfortunate effect on the adult population of our community; it has taken much of the amity out of Amityville.

De facto segregation is not peculiar to Amityville; the problem is wide-spread. But there are many authoritative guideposts to help any school board deal with their local problem, if they're sincerely interested in its resolution:

The New York State Education Department in several directives has urged school boards to eliminate de facto segregation in their community schools.

* There are a number of recent court decisions in cases that parallel our own under which school boards have been ordered to wipe out conditions of de facto segregation.

* Many communities, such as Freeport, Long Island, have worked out their own de facto segregation problems without becoming involved in court cases. These case histories are available for study and as guides for interested school boards.

* The great majority of our Nation's educational, legal, and religious authorities agree that de facto

segregation is harmful and wrong from the legal, educational and moral viewpoints.

* At the present time, our de facto segregation problem is in the courts, not because the majority of school district residents voted to handle it in this fashion, but because the Board of Education arbitrarily decided to continue the issue in the courts. As a result, our community is divided by antagonism and is receiving adverse publicity. Hundreds of our school children are educationally marking time while waiting for a court decision. Importantly, dollars which should have been spent for better education are going out for legal fees.

* Until the Northeast School issue arose, Amityville had an enviable reputation for dealing fairly and quietly with its segregation problems. I believe this present problem should, and can be, settled in the same way— fairly, quietly, and "within our own house."

* In my campaign for election to the school board, I want to give the voters of our community a chance to express themselves on this vital issue. By casting your vote for me, you will be telling the Board of Education that the Northeast School Problem should be taken out of the courts and settled at home. The Board's own Citizens' Advisory Committee has already recommended three possible solutions to the problem.

* If I fail in my campaign, the Board will know that the majority of voters, insofar as they are acquainted with the issue, support the court battle for segregation,

regardless of its cost in legal fees, community conflict, and diverse effects on the district's economy and public image.

As soon as I finished the speech, Bill said, "Mae, we've got to get out of here quick. I've been watching two sons of a gun, and I figure they plan to hurt you. It's not safe here."

Sure enough, two mornings later we were awakened to the sirens of fire trucks. The neighbors saw a big cross burning on our lawn. I told them, "The first thing I want you to do is amass a big crowd, and get the newspaper and television people into this." I wasn't frightened. I was used to that. I grew up in the South, so I knew the KKK was just a bunch of cowards. Any Black person growing up in Daytona was so used to that kind of activity.

Even so, I was scared when I had to go a meeting alone one night while Bill stayed home with Gary. I was speaking to the Darrynane Civic Association on April 26, 1964 on the issue of why Amityville children in the Northeast School do not measure up to academic standards. A copy of that speech reads:

> Children of certain neighborhoods and, therefore, those attending certain neighborhood schools, have been described variously as "culturally deprived, culturally impoverished, socially handicapped, underprivileged," and so on. Here in Amityville, children of the segregated Northeast school who do not measure up to academic standards as they go forward to the integrated classes of the fourth and fifth grades, have been described in similar terms.

As Arnold Reiners, candidate for re-election to the Board of Education, put it at the Parents Association Meet- Your-Candidate session last Thursday, these children, at the start, 'do not have the tools to do the job.' Mr. Reiners was careful to point out that this lack applies to some children 'both White and Negro.' But there was no mistaking his meaning since he offered this view as an explanation or justification of a difference in achievement between Northeast pupils and other pupils of our district. It was clear that he meant to persuade them that the fault rally lies with the children and their families.

We know, however, that the fault really lies in a mistaken attitude toward the Negro community, and also in the de facto segregation that is maintained to support this attitude.

Mr. Reiners went on to say that when pupils, either Negro or White, suffer from such handicaps, the school district must provide unequal education in the form of extra services to give them the tools they lack.

Now we must recognize that there are some children in the Northeast school, as there are in any school, who start off with handicaps. We know, too, that the majority of Northeast children do not have these handicaps. They come, rather, from middle class homes where there is adequate income, where the parents are educated, where good books and good music and good theater are cultivated, where the benefits of museums and parks and other cultural sources are promoted.

Unfortunately, in Mr. Reiner's mind, the majority of Northeast pupils are lumped together with the "culturally deprived," and this attitude is reflected in the classroom itself. Mr. Reiner cannot see that the majority are being handicapped in their education when they are treated in the same way as the few who do indeed need "special" treatment.

Yet this is surely the case when children must go through three years at Northeast at a pace geared completely to the needs of their slower classmates. The slow-up is intensified, but this time for all children, both Negro and White—when, in the fourth grade, children from Northwest and Park Avenue schools come together with the poorly prepared and insufficiently challenged children from Northeast.

The situation at Park Avenue schools today is a case in point. Here both White and Negro children are being cheated by a system that has its roots in de facto segregation. Arriving in fourth grade, the Park Avenue children find themselves in the same classes with the ill- prepared children from Northeast. By having their pace slowed down at this point to the speed of their poorly prepared classmates, they suffer precisely the same educational penalty that the Northeast children have suffered from the very first grade.

"Our school system, therefore, appears to be doing a fine job of providing tools for the "have-nots," but since nothing dulls tools like disuse, taking them away from the "haves." Under this system, and with the segregation that supports it, the North Amityville child just can't win. And the White child, of course, must share the cost.

What this speech doesn't mention is a major sore point in Amityville. To change the de facto segregation requires a busing program to other schools. The Northeast school is 90 percent Black. And it's this busing issue that engenders outrage among White racists.

The Walker printed platform also noted that "The problems that have plagued our district, resulting in wholesale resignations of teachers on all levels, continue to plague us."

After the meeting, I noticed a car with two men in it waiting for me afterwards, and they started following me home. I crossed 110 to Amityville from Crossapeake. I turned the first street going west. When I sped up, the car behind me sped up, too. As soon as I reached Glen-Malure Street I started blowing my horn. Within a minute Bill and my neighbors were turning on lights. When I pulled to my driveway, Bill was waiting outside, so the car sped on by.

When the campaign to elect me resulted in defeat, Black activists boycotted the Amityville schools over the issue of racial imbalance at the Northeast School. School Trustee Kendall Muncy made this reply to the boycott:

It is a very sorry situation when a parent sends a child to school only to have the child sent back home by one who claims to be working for the betterment of education. To keep these children, who had every intention of attending school, from their classes is to

146

defeat the claimed purpose of improving the educational standards of the children. You certainly cannot improve a child's education by depriving him of a day's schooling. I think any organization that uses this type of tactic should be severely censored by the parent of the children who were turned back.

More than 300 "more or less subdued persons" attended the next school board meeting. By this time the issue of how good the education was at Northeast had been heard to a limited extent in a Federal Court action. An application for a stay against the Amityville Board of Education was dismissed from the bench. The newspaper story about the meeting noted that "Mrs. Annie Mae Walker, a Negro who has taught in New York City for 25 years," took to task Acting District Principal Carl B. Sparke's disclosure of a case history of an emotionally disturbed child at Northeast as an example of "good education" there. (The article pointedly omits any reference to her run for the school board or her experience as an Amityville teacher for the previous four years.)

She held that Mr. Sparke was incorrect into going into a confidential case history, even though no name had been mentioned. Each speaker was allowed a theoretical two minutes of public discussion.

Views by Mrs. Bette Kersey of the board got more ink, which perhaps shows the popular White stance, as she tried to use—in reverse—the 1954 Supreme Court case (Brown Vs the Board of Education) which ended school segregation:

Now the Negro community and some White citizens in Amityville are pressuring for us to duplicate this situation by transporting White children out of their neighborhoods and assigning them to a school on the basis of color. The issue of whether it's de factor segregation and whether it's unconstitutional was not answered by the 1954 decision. This question can only be answered in the courtroom, and this board will again respect the decision of the courts.

To the critic (I was not specifically charged by name here) who calls this "legal gobbledygook, muddled thinking, poor judgment," I suggest that he or she read or reread the Preamble to the Constitution of the United States.

To the citizens who are riding on the crest of emotionalism, I should like to point out that in essence what you are saying is the end justifies the means. Need I remind you that the Third Reich was founded on the same philosophy? To those of the clergy, who support this stand, I suggest that you reexamine the morality of your position.

I continued teaching in Plainview for the 1964-65 school year. I was in Washington, D.C. attending a conference on early childhood education with Dr. Snyder when Jay Waxinburg, the principal in Great Neck, N.Y. said he had tracked me down and needed an urgent meeting. "I've never met you," he said, "but the President of the United States (Lyndon Baines Johnson) has told us to find the best person in the state to start a pre-school program available for low- income families. Everybody tells me that's you. I want you to be director of the team of researchers and create a program immediately."

I told him I was under contract and didn't need a job.

"Listen, Mae," he said, "You're the best. We have to have you. You can't refuse the President."

Editor's Notes:

Reiners, Arnold C. "Trustee's Position." Amityville Record [Long Island] 30 April 1964.

[2]. Defends Board of Education's positions and claims charges regarding de facto segregation are   spurious.

[3]_____ De Facto Segregation for Amityville Children. Darrynane, New York: Free, 1964. Charges that a neighborhood school with primarily Black students handicaps its students for life through "poor preparation and insufficient challenges" from the first grade forward in a system that "cheats all children, both Negro and white."

[4]_____ De Facto Segregation for Amityville Children. Darrynane, New York: Free, 1964. Charges that a neighborhood school with primarily Black students handicaps its students for life through "poor preparation and insufficient challenges" from the first grade forward in a system that "cheats all children, both Negro and white."

(Amityville newspaper ? date? 1)

[5] The article pointedly omits any reference to the run for the school board or experience as an Amityville teacher for the previous four years.)

[6]Ibid.

Malcolm X and Head Start

Malcolm X came to New York to create a mosque, and he had friends, Suzy and Brother Curtis, but since they didn't have extra room, he lived with us while they were raising money for and building the mosque. We gave him the spare room. Since Muslims do not use the same silverware or cooking utensils, I bought pots and dishes and silver. I was teaching while Marie Session kept my baby for me. Malcolm became so interested in my book collection. Every day, as soon as I'd open the door, he'd be right there.

"Sister, I just read this book. It's so fascinating. I did not know. . ." And then he'd start reading passages aloud before I could even sit down. He was a very pleasant person. Little Gary was just crazy about Brother Malcolm.

Then Suzy asked if Sr. Bertha could live with me. I'd finished the basement and had a parlor down there, so she also stayed. James X was living with Suzy and he had a crush on Sister Bertha. However, in Muslim culture, a man is not allowed to be alone with a single woman, so Malcolm X had to chaperone. That seemed to be fine, until just three months after Bertha and James's marriage, they had twin boys.

Brother Malcolm thought it was funny, too. When a girl gets married in that culture, she has to hang a sheet out for public view to prove she was a virgin at marriage. Malcolm would say, "Now, Bertha, you didn't hang out that sheet. You could have easily kept a rat hidden, and killed it the night of the wedding.

I went to Malcolm's services. He was preaching anti-White then. He'd say; "The White man has a way of calling Black people monkeys. But if you don't believe that it's the Whites who look like monkeys, just shave one." At one meeting, a White person tried to stab Malcolm, so then he barred Whites from the church. All Blacks had to be searched for weapons. Even women were searched. So one of those nights, I had a small pocket knife to treat ingrown toenails. But I had to give it up.

Malcolm was a beautiful, beautiful personality. We never argued because he was a Christian before Islam. He was naturally interested in all religions. I would not go so far as to say he hated Whites, but there was a lot of disapproval of relationships with Blacks. After he moved from our house, he changed religion to what he called a world view. He left the narrow view of Islams to view of Black only. He then began to allow Whites to join mosque. After he advocated brotherhood of all people, they shot him. I had been speaking at church. When I got home, Gary was crying hysterically. "They just shot my Malcolm!"

The month after Malcolm died, February 1965, Head Start offered me more money than I ever in my whole life dreamed of. So I called together a lot of educators and bureaucrats for a conference. Unfortunately, my picture was put in the paper to advertise the program. All those

White parents wouldn't send their children, they said, "to be taught by a Negro." Jay Waxinburg warned me, "They're going to crucify you."

I said we'd find Miss Jenkins, and she knew some people with money. We called a meeting of those who had registered, and I talked with them. We showed them the financial benefits of health care and dental care. I put posters all around the gym of great achievements by Black Americans. After I left those parents, they were ready to kiss me. So many people came up to me afterwards and apologized.

Do you know what we did! I got together a team of four of us: a Catholic priest, a rabbi, a Protestant minister and me. We went by foot and found seven pockets of poverty in that Great Neck area, and I wrote up a proposal for the very first Head Start.

We have to discriminate, I told them. We need a few White, blasé schoolteachers involved if we want to get public acceptance. I ran workshops to sensitize them. Right in back of the St. Regis Catholic Church, we started our program.

Great Neck had hired young Black women from the South to come as domestics. So we soon had a population of mixed race babies. For this reason, they had to cut out "renting" these 15 and 16 year-olds. Then the Whites started bringing women from Scandinavia to act as servants. The same thing happened, a lot more babies. All Catholics, they kept them hidden. Some of the children who resulted from these mixed parentages were even dwarfs, all kinds of physical ailments. Our dental cost was the greatest expenditure.

For our final program, I composed a play from Langston Hughes' poem, "What is America to me?" I gave parts to Black and White non-readers, then got all White literacy students to teach them to read. I had adults portray Frederick Douglass, Harriett Tubman, Lucretia Mott, all kinds of famous White and Black people who had worked to eliminate slavery. It was a tremendous success.

The program, exactly the way I created it, was adopted as the Head Start Model for the state of New York as well as other places in the country. The next summer Westbury, a town with even more snobbish, sophisticated people, grabbed me for their Head Start program. I got the wife of the president of the board of trustees for the school system as my coordinator. After that, I decided that the summer programs were taking too much out of me after I worked nine months in the public schools.

Hugh Cleland at the State University of New York was one of the commissioners I got to know through the NAACP. He asked me to the first woman—and the first Black woman—on the State Human Relations Commission.The commission had 12 men, two of which were Black. Immediately Mr. Dennison, the Superintendent of Suffolk County, appointed me. Nobody had considered a woman. They had been accustomed to old male mentality.

Cleland took me aside and said, "I need to talk confidentially. We need you at the University. I know you're on the top of the step at Plainview."

"I'm not ready," I told him. "Besides, I just started my doctoral program."

"Just come. We'll make you ready."

When I got to the interview with Dr. Glass, he said, "I'm going to be very honest and tell you why we have to give you more money. We started the University at Oyster Bay five years ago and agreed to train teachers, mainly in math and science. We now have five students majoring in elementary education—and not one person to supervise their program, to teach them about elementary education, or to provide teaching internships. The state of New York is going to come down like a bombshell on us."

"You can't pay as much as I'm making," I argued.

"I'm on my knees. I'm pleading," Dr. Glass said. "We'll do anything we can if you'll just write up proposal. That means teaching every subject and placing students on teaching assignments."

"I'll think about it," I said. "But what about the money? I understand the University pays peanuts."

"If you'll say you'll come and take the proposal to Albany," he promised, "I'll start you out as an assistant professor on a tenure track."

I took the bait, and they paid me $1,000 a year less than I was making as an elementary school teacher. But then they arranged a position as Consultant for Elementary Education for the State of New York. The State also granted money and special program called Academic Individual Merit for which I was in charge. Now the salary more than made up for what I'd lost. As part of my job, I'd set up workshops and offer in-service college credit classes.

The problem was that it took up all my time. Therefore, I took the job at the end of the semester. Then I engaged in writing course descriptions, being the very first woman at SUNY. I was the first Black anything. Even the janitors were White. Believe me, I had a hard time with all those men. Now they had to create a position. They made me director of elementary education so I couldn't conflict with their high and mighty chairman.

From the very first time I opened my mouth, they fought me. They just died at the notion that any woman— let alone some Black woman—would have that kind of power. They had no human feelings. I came with a brand-new outlook for students and for other people. I had it reinforced dozens of time that I was indeed inferior to these men.

One proposal involved bringing in educators from Albany. As I arrived one morning, Professor Len Gardner met me in the hall. "What the Hell do you mean bringing in a person from Albany without asking us first?"

"What the Hell do you mean accosting me!" I countered. "I'm an expert in elementary education. You're just a Johnny-Come-Lately. I will not allow you to accost me."

He backed down and apologized. After that, I didn't have overt comments. They knew I was a woman to be reckoned with—an equal, a somebody. At last!

The University Fights Back

Like David against Goliath, 27 Black students and I (the only Black faculty) faced 27,000 White students, thousands of White faculty, and an all-White administration. We needed those "slings and arrows of outrageous fortune."

Black Students United formed on April Fools Day of 1968. The crisis atmosphere which produced and surrounded the fledgling program did nothing to enhance the stated goals, including: "to provide an opportunity for better human relations" and "positive interaction." It was more like two war camps with BSU and Students for a Democratic Society on one side and the university administration on the other.

The administration's weapon was delay—put something off one year at a time and the student troublemakers may have graduated. They created a moratorium the following fall to let student organizations propose curricula and administrative changes. BSU asked for three "biggies":

1. A Black institute controlled by BSU students, faculty and outside advisors, to be set in place by September 1969. The aim was "to provide Black students with

background and educational standing necessary for them to assume the role of leadership in their community, thus eliminating the social, economic, and political problems."

2. A "Special Opportunities Program" to provide tuition, room and board, health and medical insurance, and fees for Black Students.
3. Assurance that Afro-American and Puerto Rican students would constitute no less than 25 percent of total admissions.

The administrators waited four months to even answer— then told students each part of the proposal had been turned over to five different administrative committees. A single program delegated to five separate committees could not retain unity or integrity.

What's worse—at the first meeting of committee chairs and BSU, the administrators rejected the proposed "Black Institute," but agreed to a downgraded version: a Black Studies Program. Within a week, BSU sent a letter to the President asking him to commit in writing to give first priority to hiring a director.

The President's reply totally ignored that request, just saying SUNY would look at curricular proposals for an interdisciplinary major in Black Studies. Months later, a committee selected a director and sent a letter of recommendation. Nothing happened the rest of the school year.

Next they offered to make me the first director of the first Black Studies program of any university in New York. In

July, 1969, when I received a letter of appointment, the position had been further reduced to that of Chairman. And it was stated that further "search will be conducted to find a permanent chairman of distinction from those outside our present faculty." I had been led to believe I was the permanent chairman. It took months to straighten that out.

In May I was given an office—a 9 x 12 room with no telephone. The faculty they hired turned out to be three part-time instructors who already had full-time jobs at other universities and a graduate student in the Department of Sociology. In short, I was the whole program—a chairman with no permanent help and no money. When two more rooms (without furniture) were set aside for part-time instructors, we had to yield to AIM counselors who needed the space.

But now SUNY could brag it had the first African-American studies program in New York and was committed to enabling educational opportunities for Blacks—even though between spring of 1969 and fall registration, four faculty members from the Committee for Developing Black Studies had resigned and there had been no replacement; this caused a general loss of morale about the Program. Not only that, but no advance publicity was put out and there was only one full-time faculty member present during registration. So even prospective Black students had limited advisory help.

Only six Black Studies majors were enrolled, and as a group they did not perform well academically during the semester. We can point to poor academic preparation, lack of adequate financial help, personal problems and poor tutoring as partial reasons. However, the initial members of BSU had all been high achievers. But by the time the program was in place, they were seniors and so were excluded from majoring in Black Studies.

Others might have given up. But BSU submitted a "position paper" charging that the Administration had not lived up to its promises. A lot of correspondence still produced no results. None of the demands were met.

So with traditional, peaceful procedures ignored, active protest began.

When any group emerged on campus, the Faculty Senate (of which I was a member) had to appoint a sponsor of these groups. Naturally I was appointed the sponsor of both BSU and SDS.

Soon some radical events happened--setting the chemistry building afire, for example. Students found that a lab was funded by DOW Chemical, which produced the Agent Orange used in the war with Vietnam. SDS didn't like that. BSU was angry that the state of New York furnished certain amounts of money for Black students to use their educational money for DOW chemicals. SUNY denied this, but students found important documents out at DOW and published these secret activities.

As soon as students found out things, they would secretly feed them to me. All students called me Mom. "Now you don't know anything, Mom," they'd say and grin. They staged demonstrations and boycotts. When they planned the big lock-in of University administrators in the library that closed down the university, I was also on the Human

159

Relations Commission of Suffolk County.

In 1970 I received my Ph.D. from East Coast University in Dade City, Florida, where I'd been going summers. Shortly after that, when East Coast was not accredited because of its lack of library space, SUNY gave me tests and papers to write, then awarded me another Ph.D. from there.

By this time things were hot, hot, hot in Black studies. Everything came to a head about the time my office door was set on fire. The University newspaper, *Statesman,* reported the story on March 18, 1970:

> Early Tuesday morning, in what some observers considered a political act, vandals defaced the Social Science Building office doors of Black Studies Program Director Ann Mae Walker. A circled cross sign, identified by a University policeman as a death sign, with the words "it's on you" written beneath, were scrawled in chalk on Professor Walker's door. A poster depicting the violence of the Vietnam song "My Affair" and a Black teacher's declaration, both hanging on the door, were burned to ashes. A Chicago conspiracy poster and some anti-racist cartoons were similarly set afire on the nearby office doors (1).xii

The actions drew a quick response from Black Students United. In a letter to the University Community, BSU warned:

> We, the Black community at Stony Brook, have found it necessary, at this time, to openly confront all Liberal-Conservative/ racists on campus. The administration,

faculty and students have subtly embarrassed, overtly intimidated, openly harassed, and tried to inflict violence on the Black faculty and students. This is THE FINAL WARNING TO ALL OF YOU.

The next incident perpetrated against Black people, whether small or large, will be taken as an act of open aggression against the Black community at large. AND WE WILL RETALIATE IN SELF DEFENSE.

Recent incidents include a heated argument in the Union cafeteria and a confrontation with Statesman concerning a 'bust' story. Acting President T.A. Pond released a statement late Tuesday afternoon in which he deplored the incident as a 'discredit to the entire University.'

The damage was discovered at about 7:45 a.m. Tuesday morning by Dr. Walker. She immediately called university police for aid and Education Department Chairman Eli Seifman in his office. After surveying the charred doors, he advised her to call Security.

Dr. Walker expressed profound shock at the incident. Noticeably upset, she later commented that 'what happened here is no different than what's happening all over.'

Dr. Barry Gholson, psychology professor, who has been the victim of various and unsigned obscene notes in recent weeks, saw the burned debris as an attack on the left. 'It just shows,' he said, 'what capitalism can drive people to do' (Hartman 1).

An opinion article in the same issue of the paper took a different stance: "The fact is that Black students have been provoking White students," Stu Eber wrote. "Bleeding hearts tend to ignore the push and shove, the threats at knife point and racial comments directed at Whites (Eber 1).

A front page column called the whole university a bunch of religious racists who had declared "open season" on Blacks:

> We, the Black people of this institution, do hereby recognize that you, all the White racists, have declared open season on Black people. What is permeating here at Stony Brook is simply a reflection of a nationwide trend. There were the Panthers in California, Illinois, and New York. Their destruction, both collective and individual, is an example of what the American religious White racist has in store for Black people living on borrowed ground. In the immediate racist environment of Stony Brook, youthful White racists burn crosses on the doors of Black faculty members, plus those White faculty members whose association with the Black nation implies a lucrative association and the potential missing link between the mutual institution of the White culture.

> Understand this: the Black people here at Stony Brook do not intend to be the martyrs of the seventies. This is a period in which we find transcending the current trends to be a most satisfying life-giving force. Black people are not saying that open season will be met by something which is ludicrous, barbaric and reflective of Whiteness displaced. What we are

162

saying is the open season by White racists and Black people is going to create one of the most classic examples of evolution, one which would cause Darwin to turn in his grave and tell all you other White racists to cool it, cause you are dealing with a generation that is, by nature of our teachings, prepared to transcend above and beyond the stage of martyrdom. So, White racists, you had better cool it, 'cause you can't cope with it. (Callendar 1)

The incidents followed a weekend speech to students at nearby Fredrick Douglass College, by Black congresswoman Shirley Chisholm:

All up and down this land there is a veritable social revolution going on: Black people are asking for their share of the American Dream, whatever that dream may be. Women, as well, are now rising to ask for a proper share, while the young are questioning the very values on which the American society is based.

But as the schism grew and the fire of racial hatred flared up, the truth is I was getting too hot for the University to handle. Soon after the door burning incident, J. Bentley Glass, the academic vice president at SUNY and a board member of the Danforth Foundation gave me a call. "Mae, guess what! You've just been named a Danforth Scholar. You're off to Berkeley or Yale. You can pack your bags and pick your choice. "

163

Editor's Notes:

"Open Letter: All Administrators of State University at
Stony Brook," Black Students United, Feb.7, 1969. Quoted
in The Implementation and Development of
Interdisciplinary Programs in Black Studies in the
University. Dissertation by Annie Mae McClary Walker,
East Coast University, August 1970.

[2]Letter of appointment, John S. Toll, President, July 23,
1969.

Maya Angelou and the 'Great Queen'

My first choice was Berkeley. Everything was swinging there. But my husband could come see me on Sunday at Yale. Also I knew Yale had never had a Black woman fellow, and only four of the 22 Danforth Fellows were women.

I soon learned that professors at Yale are unlike any other place in the world. I had John Thomson and Basil Davidson, who established Black universities in Africa. Besides, I was somebody special that year. I courted them for their knowledge. I had a good time. I could invite anybody I wanted.

Because there was no place for Blacks to stay, it took Yale a year to find housing. When the university invited Maya Angelou to come for an extended seminar, my apartment was the only place in town where she could stay. I had a see-through fireplace with living rooms on both sides of it. Maya Angelou was so down-to-earth and informal. We sat up late at night talking about our personal histories.

All year I could work with students and faculty in Black history. I didn't just eat it up, I gulped it! Naturally I made A's, because I loved to talk about Black history. Once I walked into the first class late and the professor just stopped his lecture cold. "An Oshun has come in. I can tell. Will the Oshun meet me for lunch after class?"

He was right. I was first initiated into the tribe in Oshlongoo, Nigeria. Here the religion is incorrectly called voo doo and people think it's just sticking pins in dolls. But it's much more than that. Any time people have tried to take pictures of Yoruba rites, they find that cameras don't work. They would blow up.

I'm Oshun, one of the Orishias, which people refer to as gods, but really they are not Gods. If they are, they are lesser gods. The Yoruba religion is very much like Catholicism, where there is a Supreme Being who we call God; the Yorubas call him Voodoo or Voodoon. Then there is Voodoo's son, Obatala. After Obatala, who is the equivalent of Jesus Christ, comes Yemena, the dark blue and White beads. She would be the equivalent of Mary in Catholicism.

Once you're initiated, you get all the beads. When you're ready for the seventh bead, it's called Ogun, dark green and Black, which means iron. Every Yoruba rides around with something iron in his or her car. That saves them from serious damage. Ogun is the protector. Westerners call a gun a thing that you shoot. But Yorubas don't use iron to hurt people. You use it for sculptures or things to protect you.

Not until you get the seventh bead do you get initiated. Then you take more steps to becoming a priestess. I never had time to do that because I was too anxious to finish the work for my doctorate, but I knew the steps I would take.

In Yoruba, Shango, the thunder god, who would hurl thunderbolts to strike in bad places, is married to Oshun. When he married Oshun, he developed a different personality. It's a beautiful religion.

My friend Judith Gleason, who is White and Irish, also an anthropologist at Columbia University and writer of several books, went through the training with me. For seven nights we slept on the floor and had to eat the foods they fed us, some of which we didn't like. We had to eat it without complaining, and we had teaching from Suzanne Wenger, a European artist who has created a monument to the goddess Oshun, and Shunta all day long. Shunta, the priestess, was Puerto Rican; Pancho, the priest, was Cuban. Bill came over to Nigeria for my initiation. You talk about being prophets or having what we call the eye; well, these really had it. I used to ask Suzanne, "How did you get into this? Here you are White and blond and you come from Holland.

"Mae, you will learn that this is a religion who doesn't exclude anybody. It doesn't know anything about Black or White or other colors."

I remember now that doing background on my father, I found that his family had origins in Yoruba. Maybe this is why he felt the way he does about people, and felt that anyone who would stoop so low as to hate someone had something wrong with his head.

You should have seen Bobalua, Suzanne's husband; he was six foot and darker than midnight, and he would come only when he had business with Suzanne, for she was the head wife. He stayed there with her. The other times he would make his rounds with his other wives.

There are several forms of divination. The one we used, in Efe, is that divination comes about by using pieces of coconut or coral shells or little rocks, and that's how you get your name. My name, Iya Olabumi, means the great one, the great queen. I have several books on Yoruba and meanings. You select one for yourself: Melville Herkeitzh, a White anthropologist, wrote about the Yoruba religion and relationship to Catholicism. (*Myth of the Negro,* late 40's or *New World Negro,* published in the 60's.) He's the one who showed how the priests of Yoruba still exist in the Black church today. You know—when people become possessed and throw the fan up in the air—that's part of it.

When I became inititiated along with Judith, I said to her, "I'm going to tell Suzanne that I'm not going to act like a fool like some of these people. When they dance to the Orisha, I'm not going to pass out. I know I'm not." Bill was there, and he said, "Want to bet?"

I said, "No, I'm not going to do it. You watch." Well I started dancing to Oshun. Everyone has a certain step, and I was dancing, oh, was I having a good time. I don't know when I passed out. All I knew is I was sitting over in a chair in the right hand corner of the room. Shunta was on one side of me, blowing in my ear, and she said to Bill, "Blow in this ear."

"Who am I—and what's happening?" I asked. They all laughed at me. "Oh, sure, you're not going to pass out, you're not going to become possessed. But you did."

When it came Judith's time, right after me, she said "Mae, I don't think I can hold to what I said. After seeing you, I can't make promises not to pass out." Sure enough, she did. Judith was a Yemenga, and when they started playing her song, she had on a gali that must have been eight or nine yards of cloth wrapped around her. As she danced, it began to unwind. I started to touch it, but the priest and priestess warned me, "No! Don't touch it. If you touch anything on her now, you'll become possessed."

Judith was out for a long, long time. But when she came to, I took her hand and said, "Now we are both truly Yorubas.

According to Yoruba history, Oshun is an old orisha, a protectress who was present before kings, conquerors and empires. She is "the water of life, the force which every other orisha has to receive from her. Ambivalently, Oshun is both seen as the young woman, the velvet-skinned concubine and as the ancient woman steeped in magic. She is the concubine, desirable and seductive—because her life-giving force must be accessible to all. She is also the tyrannical, dominant woman, enabling her male worshippers to be secretly relieved in their inner-most hearts that in this one relationship, they need not take the initiative. Oshun gives children, cures disease and is capable of fulfilling all wishes."

My American Priestess, Shanto, had a big house in the Bronx with a big basement, and once a month she would have ceremonies there. I went there and there were people from all over Africa and Brazil and European countries. I remember this White woman there who said, "This is the most beautiful experience I've ever had in my life, finding people of all races and all nationalities here together enjoying the same thing and dancing to the Orishas. Usually priestesses don't get possessed, but that day she was dancing alone. She was dancing and all of a sudden she started shaking. A man went over to help her, but the others warned him, "Don't touch. Don't touch!" Even so a little girl touched her garment.

You should see the guys in Brazil jumping on broken glass and not get a cut. You see that in Bermuda, too, when they jump on the hot coals. When we came back to a funeral of some of the priest's family or friends, the Orishas were having a ceremony, and they couldn't notify him because he wasn't there; therefore, he broke up the whole thing. So any time they have a service, they have to put an iron pot at the door. The iron pot has all the symbols of Jesus Christ. They have to put food in the pot, chicken or any kind of meat, but not chicken necks or feet—that would be an insult to Him. But that has to be there before anybody else can come in.

Editor's note: [Mae brought a small iron pot out of her bedroom closet]. These are seven tools of Christ. There's a mallet, a hoe, a measure, (what are others?). These are what you get when you become Ocha, the final stage of study, and you know who your Orishas are. A child doesn't have to go through this. After you make Ocha, you make Ogun, one of the Orishas, and get this last bead.

Obalata represents Jesus Christ. (Alice Walker's husband was Obatela). After that comes Elegba or Eshu (either name), who's good and bad. His head is shaped like a penis. If you do something bad to him, he will pounce on you. If you're good, he will reward you. Next comes Shango, the one who hurls stones, the thunder and lightning bolts. But before him comes his first wife, Yemenga, and fans the elements, brings up the storm for him to act upon it. And after that comes Demecca, Oshango—I forgot what his job was, but he's pretty much a calm person. He's a con artist. And then comes Ogun, iron, so if anybody's bothering you, all you have do is hold up your iron. And then you call Shango to come hurl some lightning. And he'll call Yemenga and tell her to out and fan the elements so it will rain or storm.

After Bill got into the religion, one day I was out working in the garden at Stony Brook and I had him helping. He didn't really like it, so he went to sit down and said, "Mae, would you please tell Shango to let me alone and let me rest? I'm really tired."

"Well call upon Elegba," I answered. "And he'll put Shango in his place."

They pray upon this [small iron pot] and bless it. But until you reach this stage of Ocha, you are a junior priestess. Periodically I'm supposed to feed this guy, Elegba, like Peter. He's the gatekeeper. I feed him real food, put it in this dish. You imagine that he eats it. Then it sits on an altar. I was lucky enough to have red and Black, his colors. Esau is a Biblical name. He tore that building up when he was invited to the ceremony. Voodoo is the name of the deity, the holy one. People say that's a practice of witchcraft, but it really isn't. It's a religion. Where we say God, they say Voodoon; where we say Obatala, meaning pure and good, it means Jesus Christ. And I think Shango is like St. Christopher or St. Jude, one of the saints. You can do the same thing for this Orisha, pray for peace and harmony.

After I read about John Griffith's death, (Black, Like Me) Lord, did I cry. You know he died of cancer using that lamp to give him ultraviolet rays. He risked his life to prove a point. He was an anthropologist, too. He also used injections to give him dark, dark coloring. That's what gave him melanoma. But he lived that life. And he proved his point. That's where I got my inspiration for this poem.

Here's a poem I wrote, using my Yoruba name, which is a bit insulting to White people:

Blackness is
What Blackness Does

By Iya Olabunmi (Mae McClary Walker)
4/8/74

Blackness is a product of the Sun. . .

Created by the Sun's rays
For every living thing:
Plants and Animals,
Especially Non-Black people,
Depend upon the Sun for coloring.

Blackness receives

Color
Vitality
Exuberance
Beauty,
Unmatchable properties
From the Sun.

Blackness sheds its enticing, envious gleam

Upon millions of non-Black people
Who spend millions of Black-exploited dollars
Traveling to distant places
To bask in the Sun
To get blessed with Blackness!

But Sun-baskers don't know the secret of Blackness:
Blackness, like a River, is three dimensional. . .

Still, gentle, warm, inviting;
Dignified, though temperamental;
Arrogant and determined to follow
Its own course, regardless of obstacles:
Rough, tough, turbulent, uncontrollable,
It can devour its would-be obstructers.

Blackness, like a River,

Is that irrepressible and immovable force
Endowed and commissioned by the Sun

To be a partner,
To give substance and sustenance
For coloring, living, and growing
Persons and things.

Blackness is the source

From whence comes Love,
From whence comes Passion,
From whence comes Beauty
From whence comes Creativity
And all Spiritual vibrations
For the Planet Earth.

Off to Africa and Beyond

I investigated Bill's s educational benefits through the GI Bill. I also managed to get him a full scholarship to the School of Social Welfare at SUNY. Sure enough, they paid Bill's tuition and he went on to finish his master's degree in social welfare. He went from high school to getting a M.S.W. in just three years by working six days a week. I helped him with his studies by assigning my graduate students to do research for his thesis, and I typed the thesis. Meanwhile, he went on to take two more courses with me.

Bill graduated with in 1976, and immediately got a job working at Central Islip Hospital, then Pilgrim State Hospital. His job was to place hospital patients into half-way houses in private homes. He also had to prepare them to live in a home after spending years in a state mental institution.

At the same time Gary was in college at Jackson State, Mississippi, taking classes with Alice Walker (*The Color Purple*), and through him, I got to know her, too. He finished a whole semester ahead of his class there.

Bill always insisted on introducing me as his wife, Dr. Walker. If someone called and asked for Mrs. Walker, Bill would say, "Which one of the Mrs. Walkers do you want?" He told me, "I want them to address you by your proper title. You worked so hard to earn it."

In 1970, I finished my Ph.D. at East Coast University and was teaching at Stony Brook. A year after that, the State took away East Coast's accreditation. But since SUNY had underwritten that degree, they made good on it and had me pass some exams and write papers; then they gave me the Ph.D. degree from the State University of New York.

After I finished the Danforth year at Yale, I was sent to Ghana in 1972, where I was invited by the Prime Minister to greet the Black Olympians. Shirley Temple Black stood on one side of me and the Prime Minister on the other. He could greet each person in his own language. I felt very humble that I could just speak 10 languages (English, Latin, French, Spanish, Italian, Efe, Yoruba, Kiswahalie, Ewe, and Ashanti).

Knowing both sides of my family in our history experienced violence and harsh treatment, through no fault of their own, resulted in bitterness that is an admitted and fundamental part of my personality. However, it also means I don't believe in violence as a solution. I am committed to work endlessly in the liberating struggle for my people

I became a friend in Liberia with Chinua Achebe, the author of Things *Fall Apart*. I think he got Pulitzer Prize for that. I wrote a question in this volume he gave me in Monrovia: "Is it possible for a man to gain knowledge of who he is, that is his identity, his sense of greatness or weakness, through independent thought by which he determines his actions, or must he depend upon the collective thoughts and opinions of his clansmen or a determination of his actions through which his true identity is revealed?" I read this over and over. The answer to this question is still pending. I still would like to find the answer.

Blacks are quite willing to denounce other Blacks because of their association in groups. In fact, Blacks always seem to be more judgmental of other Blacks than White people are. In my anthropology classes the Blacks sit there frowning and disapproving and rejecting social activities of the Masai people or when I talk of activities like the Yamama people who Indians in Northern Brazil and that sort of thing, whereas the White students by and large accept them—or at least don't prejudge them. I don't find the ethnocentrism so typical of Blacks.

At the beginning of every semester I have students memorize the concept of ethnocentrism and multi-culturalism and give them examples of other cultures that do things differently from us, particularly in the realm of sex. The Black students squirm uncomfortably, but White students accept things and appreciate these difference.

For example, I tell them that with the Eskimos of the far North the ultimate act of courtesy is for the husband of the igloo to offer his wife to "laugh in" with a male visitor. In preparation the wife has to bathe herself in urine which is stale, that's been sitting a long time, adorn her hair in blubber oil, and that oil is old and stinky, but she's preparing for the "laugh in." I say, "How many of you on your honeymoon would go in the bathroom and use toilet water before you got in bed? Well, that's what she did. She used toilet water." That's cultural relativism.

Once a young priest came to this village and the Eskimo made provisions for his wife to "laugh in" with him and took the children away. He hadn't gone very far when the husband heard this screaming from priest—complaining the man's wife was pulling on him. The father ran back, leaving the children, and bashed that priest's head against the ice wall until he died--because he had snubbed the highest act of courtesy with his wife. Isn't that something! The White students understand that perfectly; the Black students shake their heads and jeer.

In that same village, when the daughter marries, the mother moves in with the young couple for the express purpose of chewing leather with her teeth, making it pliable enough to sew for clothing or something like a shade to insulate a window. When her teeth are worn down to the gum and she can no longer tan the leather, it is her ardent request that she be taken out and sat on a block of ice and be left there to die and let the vultures pick the flesh from her body.

I ask the students, what is relevant in our culture? They said, we take the elderly when they get useless to a nursing home to be left there to die. That's our cultural relevancy. Once again Black students recoil. They think that's cruel. That's mean. I couldn't do my mother or grandmother that way. And that's the difference between Black and White reactions still.

I think the students are shocked that I don't use the term "illegitimate." But as I said before, "There's nothing either legitimate or illegitimate about intercourse, and teach them to use a less stigmatized term, 'out of wedlock.'"

In telling students about my experience with the Yoruba, and acquiring a lot of their practices, the Blacks think that's horrible. They think of voodoo only as making a little wooden doll and sticking pins in it; they don't think of it as a religion. But it is a religion, and the word voodoo— or voodorn--means god or deity. In this country, and in Haiti and Jamaica, they call it hoo doo, but it's the same thing.

Black Americans, therefore, often find it impossible to accept customs of other lands. Take my friend GloriaWright who came to me from Long Island, New York, sort of a temperamental devil, one of the Cinneqoit Indian girls, but I met her in Liberia and we just fell in love with each other right away. And one day when most of the people from the University had gone on a field trip, I didn't feel well. She called that morning and found out I was home. She taught in the English sector between grade school and high school. She took off that day and took me to various bookstores. Oh, the books that girl bought for me I'd never heard of. This was one of them.

Her husband, Col. Wright, was one of those thirteen men in '78 or '79 that they lined up in Liberia and shot, but she was already here. She'd left him because he did her a dirty deal, a rotten deal. He was a member of the Krew tribe. They believed in Islamic religion, along the East Africans. Most of them are Islamic. His first wife died; she had identical twin boys and two girls and a baby. The youngest was only six months old. This was Gloria's second African husband. Well, she raised this kid.

When this husband left her, the boy was thirteen years old. That was her baby. She never had any children of her own. He walked in one day and did what the other Muslims do.

He said three times, "I divorce you once. I divorce you twice. I divorce you three times." That means you have to get going, leave everything, children, personal belongings, everything.

What she said to him was, "You forget that I am from the United States of America, and you don't throw me out with nothing. I struggled and raised these children. These children are mine."

So he said, "What will you have of me?"

"I will have a house. Matter of fact I'll have two." She did. He built her a mansion. So when I went to Liberia, I asked the taxi driver to take me to Gloria Wright's house, and when we got there, he blew that horn. You do not get out of the car there without blowing the horn. Along came two big German Shepherds, one from this side and one from the other. At the same time a voice came over the loud speaker, "Who are you and what do you want here?"

He said, "This is Dr. Walker, Gloria's friend from the States."

"Oh, yes. Bring them in," she said. I had Catherine Cook, who was a cousin to Gloria's ex-husband. She came out to the car to help me out. I don't know why she always calls me Maya. She said, "Maya, I'm so glad to see you, and you can come in." But she also said, "Catherine, you can't come into my house."

She said, "Please, Gloria. Let me come in and tell you what happened." That was between Catherine and Gloria's sister here in the States. So I pleaded, "Gloria, please let her in because she came with me all the way from the states."

Gloria said, "Okay, but I have to take her in and talk to her before I talk to you."

She took that girl in the room, and she came out crying. Gloria said, "Don't cry any more. I'll have the servants bring you some food." She had two servants on one side of the house and two on the other side. The men do the work all throughout Africa, all the housework and all the cooking. The wives and children just stay in the place provided for them.

We were all going to a wedding that evening. You know about the Liberia Colony. That was the first colony in Africa that was owned by anybody outside of Africa. That was United States, the only colony of the U.S. It was chartered in 1822, and got its independence in 1847. That came about because somebody, Francis Scott Key "Oh Say Can You See," Frances Scott Key, chairman of African Colonization Society — I wrote a poem about him. I'll look up.

I don't have too much respect for old mister "Oh Say Can you See." So all of these people sent back to Africa were free Blacks. And the free Blacks had become a threat to the slave system, and particularly after the uprising between the Seminoles and the American government, so colonists in America felt it was better to send free Blacks back to Africa and colonize them than to have to tolerate them here.

And we had such people as David Walker in 1829, to Nat Turner, 1832,Rush Worn, Martin Vessey, Gabriel Prosser, all these people who were fighting slave holders in America for what they had done to Black people here. And their insistence that the slaves on the plantations were getting from free Blacks. They had to have haircuts, right? And they had to have medical service and other service. Nobody from White race was going to do those things, so colonists had to depend on free Black professionals, and there were a number of them here. Right and left they were writing slaves passes, because every Black person had to have a pass. It was a good thing that it was felt they all looked alike. Some of the free Blacks would give the slave Blacks their passes. If a Black man was caught without a pass or snapshot, he could be imprisoned and sold back into slavery. They had a posse of fugitive hunters.

The American Colonization Society with Keyes started in 1818. By 1822, they had chartered their boats and gotten a stamp of approval to take free Blacks back to Africa to colonize them. That's why Tubman was president until fairly recent years, because he was a relative of Harriett Tubman. And you have names like Wright, like my friend Gloria. The AME church often sends speakers over there. That was what I was on—a mission to speak to the people, and teach them something about their American heritage.

In 73, I was a visiting professor at the University of Dar es Salaam, Tanzania, and Bill went with me for a semester. I was doing field studies with the Muslim groups. Not one of the four would talk to or even associate with one of the other groups. That's always been so hard for me to understand. Though the British now have the public school where all children are compelled to go, groups do not mix walking to and from school. There are the Arab Muslims, the Asian Muslims, mainly from India, the Afro-Asians, and the native African Muslims, which are by far the largest group and the one much more dedicated to their religion. They carry little prayer rugs folded like a newspaper under their arm, then stop wherever they are seven times a day to kneel and pray on their mat.

It was ungodly hot in December and January, an average temperature of 110 degrees with no air conditioning. So we had to open our bedroom window a little to get some of that stagnant, stale, humid air—even though the window opened right next to the courtyard of an African-Asian mosque. Every night I'd hear the drum beats start up about 2 a.m. and go darum, adrum, rum all night long.

You wonder how sincere people can be, claiming to be so religious and still refusing to sit next to their neighbor. When they go to Mecca, that's in Asia for Ramadan once a year, they sit on the train with their backs to each other, not speaking. Such contradiction. Lovely people to me, though.

The last time I was in Ghana was as a visiting professor at the University of Magoon. Because of the heat and humidity, no classes met after 12. It was so hot you could wash clothes at noon and have them dry on the line an hour later.

One day I was sitting with two students in the Chinese pavilion when I noticed a lovely, lovely woman staring at me as she walked a few steps behind her husband. If my sister Susie were not dead, I'd swear this was she. The resemblance was uncanny.

She stepped out in front of the man. "Do you know why I'm staring at you?" she asked. "You look exactly like my sister. You look like me. Therefore, I am certain I want to ask you this question. Will you please marry my husband?"

Well, first of all I didn't find him sexually appealing. "I can't," I explained. "I am already married."

"That doesn't make any difference here," her husband retorted. "I'm a lawyer and a judge. I can divorce you. And I want to marry you."

"I can't and I won't," I declared.

"If I say so here, you do," he said. And now I was in a jam, because one cannot insult an elder in that country.

His wife gave me more reasons. "I'm a mid-wife and have to be gone a lot. My husband has to have his sex satisfaction. Before I found a young woman," she continued. "But now she has two children nursing and isn't available."

"Look lady," I said. "I'm wearing a wedding ring."

"Oh, I can divorce you in a matter of minutes," the Judge shrugged.

Suddenly I knew how to solve the problem. "I'm older than you. So if I marry your husband, I get to be the first wife— not you. Besides, do you know that Florida women carry razors or switchblade knives inside our stockings? If you interfere, I'll cut you. Besides, since I'm older, you'll have to leave. That's our social life. We don't share our men."

Nobody—but nobody—insults or angers an elder. So I got out of that!

A New Book
A Terminal Diagnosis

When I came back to Stony Brook in 1974, I wasn't feeling well. I was busy working on my first major textbook, *The Education of Afro-Americans in America*, which was finally published in 1976. My back was really bothering me. I went from one doctor to another, until I got a diagnosis of cancer. At that point I went to Sloan-Kettering Cancer Center, which was supposed to be the best in the county.

On Dec.17, 1976, the doctor called Bill and me into his office to tell us some news, "which isn't too good." He said I had osteosarcoma, cancer of the spine, and that I would need to take chemotherapy.   Bill asked the question I couldn't: "Will this cure the cancer?"

"There's no known cure for this type of cancer," the doctor answered.

"Then how long do I have to live?"

"The maximum life expectancy is about six months," he said. "You need to make a will and do everything now you've wanted to do."

Instead I had to take disability for a year and a half and stayed in home traction that whole period. All my hair fell out from the chemotherapy, of course. It was a scary, very painful time.

While I was at home, ABC TV asked me to write a two-hour special documentary on the history of black churches in America, a subject which had always been close to my heart. When I think of the burnings going on now throughout the South, I realize that racists still see black churches as a threat to their subversive causes.

Black churches were born out of struggle, and have always been havens in times of civil unrest. That's where spirituals were born.   How these spoke of longings and suffering. But they were also messages to people who could understand the real meaning behind them.   For example, "All God's children got shoes" was sung in reference to the underground railroad taking slaves to freedom. "Swing Low Sweet Chariot" meant that Harriet Tubman (Black Moses) was on her way. The slave women were big pleated skirts with aprons because those were safe places for slaves to be hiding.   So while Master and Missus smiled as the slaves sang, thinking that meant they were happy, right in front of them, other slaves were crawling from one skirt to under another out to the wagons.   The poor whites drove the wagons because they wanted slaves out of the South so they could get work.

The black church was founded in the early 1750's. The Baptists began with George Liele from Jamacia, who had a very small following. After the Civil War, after 1882 when the Yankees pulled out, things got bad for Blacks.

Instead of paying me for the script, ABC sent me four tickets to see "Porgy and Bess" on Broadway, a play which I'd already seen a number of times. I did get my interviews shown on TV, and I sold my house to move to Florida the same day the show was aired.

SUNY had promoted me to an associate professor because I hadn't enough publications yet to make full professor. By the time my major book came out the next year, I decided to retire and make use of whatever time Bill and I had left to come back down to Florida.

When I retired from Stony Brook, the university gave me all the equipment I had in my office, so I got to bring one of the three electric typewriters. My secretary called me "Ma", too. They also gave me that map of Africa I have hanging up. My students gave me that.

On March 17, 1977, Bill and I moved back to Florida, though our new house in Deltona wasn't ready yet. One day we traveled from Dade City and rode down to find my old homestead and my mother's grave. I remembered the old phosphate mine in the back yard. When Bill and I went back, I didn't see another house on the street. But at the end of the street was a little depot. This old man at the depot said, "You go up two miles and turn right. Go across the overpass. Then you'll see a place called Mounds. Your mother's grave would be the second one on the right."

We found the place with no trouble. But people had always told us, "Nobody gets into Indian mound." The restaurant tried to tell us where they thought the entrance was. But when we neared there, the most God-awful storm came up.

I told Bill. "This is not a legend. This is the truth." We never found our way inside the burial ground.

Shortly after we moved into our new house, we had our first fire. Gary was on leave from his station in Jersey and came here and left Gina, his wife, sleeping on the sofa. We met him coming in after he'd stayed out all night. We were going fishing at Monroe Lake. The night before, when he left, I'd made chicken and potato salad, a whole lot of stuff. When we were fishing, I saw this car drive up, and I said, "Dad, that's Gina in the car. I wonder what's wrong."

She jumped out and said, "Ma, you'll have to come home. There's been a fire in your house." Gary had come home, put a frying pan on the stove, then went into the bathroom and fell sleep. He'd been drinking and passed out. Gina woke up when she heard the fire engines coming. Some neighbor saw the blaze and called the fire department.

Naturally that was the same day that Dr, Oswald Bronson, the new president of Bethune-Cookman College, and his wife decided to drop by to visit us. When Helen arrived, she said, "I smell smoke."

I explained Gary had set our brand new house afire. But was I lucky again. That's the last time it was painted. That was a good paint job. But again we were lucky enough to have new cabinets available to fit our kitchen, and we had to get all new appliances. And this man charged just $3,500 to clean our whole house. Gary did this, and then he went on back.

Bill and I both started teaching as adjunct instructors at Bethune-Cookman. I couldn't work full time because Social Security didn't allow me to earn more than $7,500 a year. The new dean took an instant disliking to me, and vice versa. Even knowing that I had cancer of the spine and walking was painful for me, this woman deliberately put me into third floor classrooms, which had no elevator access. Bill continued to teach criminal justice and a sociology course, but I couldn't take the steps. I quit after the first semester.

In January of 1978, Gary and Gina came down. "Mother, I don't like the way you wear your hair, bunched up in a bun like that," Gina said. So she took me to the beauty shop at Belk-Lindsey. When I came back to the house, I saw cars parked as far as I could see. I thought somebody was having a mighty big party. When Gina and I came inside the front door, Dave Anderson and his fiancé met us at the door.

"What the devil are you two here for?" I asked. Then Dr. Watson handed me champagne, and a whole house full of people, most of the faculty of Bethune-Cookman and most of my cousins sang out "Happy Birthday." Bill had got my cousin Margaret to buy chicken, Dr. Watson had filled up the shed with coolers of champagne. Before we ate, Bill Dunn's wife brought out a mink stole. We danced to taped music and had a great time.

Later I asked Bill how he was able to afford a mink stole. "First I called Sue to borrow $200 to put down," he said. Then I told the Betty Dreyfus store I'd pay $300 down and the other $400 on installments. She said yes."

I didn't remind him that it's never cold enough to wear mink in Florida. We just paid off those installments, and he felt happy he could give me such a generous gift.

After little Gary, our grandson, was three years old, he invited us to come to Grandparents Day at the Twinkle Star preschool in DeLand. I jumped at the opportunity. We sat with our grandson, and I was so impressed at lunch that the children served themselves. Everyone was asked by the director to do an evaluation. After she read my evaluation, both Bill and I were asked to serve on the board of directors. I also wrote up the background of Maria Montessori, too, since the school used Montessori methods. Bill and I were on the board about five or six years, and I took her five people there who are still on the board.

Finally Bill's illness forced our resignation. After that, Regina asked me to be the graduation speaker. I took words of "Twinkle, Twinkle Little Star" and adapted them to rhyme with "Montessori is what we are." I used one of the Spanish teachers to teach the Spanish version to the children. I used the text, "We build the ladder by which we climb." We had ladder stepping. Very dramatic and moving. Everybody loved it. It gave me a chance to learn more about Maria Montessori, too.

In 1979 I went over to the local campus of the community college to inquire about taking piano lessons. But when the dean, Jeanne Field, heard about my background from the receptionist who'd asked me to fill out forms, she summoned me to her office.

"Here's a contract, and you will teach social studies for us," she said.

I started to object about being retired and in ill health.

"There will be no discussion," Field said. "Sign right here."

That's the moment I fell for her. She was my kind of woman. I hadn't been teaching there long when I told Jeanne I'd follow her wherever she went and teach for her as long as she'd have me.

I'd been taking Laetrile, which is vitamin 17, for my cancer while I was in New York. But when I went to see an orthopod in DeLand, Dr. Dick Huster went into the bathroom at the office and dumped it all down the toilet. He said it wasn't allowed in Florida. He referred me to Dr. Weigam and Bill to his partner, Dr.Shefry.

Bill's doctor sent him into the hospital immediately for a heart triple by-pass, and told him to take it easy. He was 68. So Bill retired from BCC, too, and took a job as night watchman at the Central Florida Regional Hospital. Then Bill had two heart attacks fifteen days apart and the aneurysm thing where he fell and blacked out. He insisted on chauffeuring me to teach at Daytona Beach Community College in New Smyrna Beach. He'd lift that heavy wheel chair in and out of the car for me when he was sicker than I was.

In 1988, we went back to New York for me to accept an honorary doctorate of letters at Bank Street College. I thought it would be a good idea to go back to Sloan-

Kettering and have a check-up for my cancer. Do you know my doctor called out the entire staff to come see me. "This woman is a living miracle," he said. "There's no way she should be alive, let alone walk in here 12 years after we told her she had just a few months to live."

In 1995, Bill's personality began to change. Sometimes when I'd lie awake sobbing at night because the pain was so bad in my legs, Bill would complain I was keeping him awake. He'd never done that before. In recent times, four or five times Bill was ill in the night. The last time when he fell in the bathroom, I couldn't talk on the phone either. I was so out of breath when I called 911 to tell them to send an ambulance.

"Is he breathing?" the woman on the phone asked.

"I don't know. While I'm wasting time talking to you, maybe he's stopped."

"Get hold of yourself," she said. "Otherwise, we'll have to come for you, too."

She told me she'd already dispatched the call to the police, so I should go to the door and blink the lights so they could see the house clearly. In a matter of minutes, they were there.

It scared me to death. Oh, Lord, I was in bed. I saw him sitting in the bathroom and I called out, "Dad, what's the matter?"

"Oh, nothing," he said, so I went back to sleep. All of a sudden I heard this "Whumph!" I sat bolt upright, turned on the light and saw Bill had fallen halfway between the bed and the bathroom. He was still.

I called my cousin, Lorenza, and he came right over. When we got to the hospital, everybody came to see about Bill. He knew everybody on the staff because he worked there seven or eight years as the night security guard. The male nurse said, "Bill, what are you doing here again?" He said he didn't know.

He talked a lot in Dr. Weigam's office that last day. He'd just been out of the hospital one day, Christmas Day, and he didn't want to go back. Gary put him in my wheelchair to go to the doctor's office. When Bill and I were alone with the doctor, Dr. Weigam asked Bill what day it was. Bill looked at me and said, "I don't know. Beats me. Ma, you tell him."

"Bill, what holiday did we just celebrate?"

Bill just looked at me again and shook his head. Dr. Weigam began singing, "Rudolph the Red Nose Reindeer" and then "Silent Night." "Any of that familiar to you?"

Bill said no.

"I guess today's the second," Bill said

"The second of what?"

"I have no idea," Bill said. "You're going to have to get all your information from my wife." Bill just laughed.

When the doctor asked Bill if the hospital gave him any medicine, Bill again didn't know, so we called in Gary, who was carrying the bottle in his pocket. Gary gave the pills to Jody, the nurse, to give to Bill, but Bill couldn't swallow. The water kept going out. So he said, "OK, Jody, let him alone right now."

Gary was standing right behind him and said, "Dad, I didn't know until I looked on the hospital chart that Mom was older than you. She's a dirty old woman who robbed the cradle."

"Bill laughed and looked up at me. "Yeah, you're a dirty old woman who robbed the cradle."

Then Dr. Weigam said he'd have to send Bill back to the hospital and asked Bill where he wanted to go.

"I want to go back to my hospital," he said. "Call an ambulance. I'll need oxygen."

The doctor went outside the door. Then all of a sudden I heard Bill gasp three very hard breaths. Then his arms flew straight up, and he fell back against Gary's arms. He was gone.

Dr. Weigam came in, the woman attendant came in and put the stethoscope against his chest. "I don't get any pulse."

The man attendant wanted to give Bill resuscitation.

"No," Dr. Weigam said. "You will not do that in my office. I am the doctor, and this man has been my patient fifteen years." He was mad. About that time, I let out a scream.

Dr. Weigam left every one of them, and came over and knelt at my feet and took my hands. "Mae, you know I've done the best I could all these years."

And he had. He had told me the Friday before that Bill was going to die, that his body was just worn out. I was so upset I stayed up all night writing the obituary and a tribute to my husband. I felt that was what I should do.

At the funeral, Verla Mae sang Bill's favorite hymn, "Precious Lord, Take My Hand." The president of Bethune Cookman came back from a family vacation in Colorado to speak at the service. The vice president of Daytona Beach Community College and Jeanne Field, the dean of South campus and a close personal friend, were among those who commemorated Bill's life.

Now, every time I remember Bill throwing up his arms, I have myself a screaming good time in this house. I miss Bill so. I can't stay here under any circumstances. People tell me, the house is nearly paid for, why don't you stay? But I don't want to stay. I was here with Bill, and this house isn't the same without my Bill. Bill was a good person; he was a kind man; he was a thoughtful man. Bill loved me with a passion. Everybody knew that.

They threw out the pattern when Bill was made. He was the gentlest, the kindest, the most affectionate man I've ever met in my whole life. He absolutely adored me. He'd say, "You're the greatest woman I've ever met." He really did. I miss him so. Oh, how I miss him.

Home at Last

When we came back in '77, St. Patrick's Day, I introduced Wendell to Bill, and after that, he'd always call and say, "Please, Mr. Walker, will you take me such and such a place?" Not only that, but Bill did it cheerfully. That's one man in a million. Every fourth Sunday all of us sat down to dinner together at his sister Ophelia's house. I expected Wendell to be uptight, but because he had three sisters who depended so much on Bill, everything went well. She'd put me in between Wendell and Bill. One day I said, "Sister, this is deliberate seating. This is no accident."

"Of course, it's deliberate," she replied. "After all, they're both your husbands."

Bill didn't care. He never let anything bother him. When Wendell died of a heart attack, Bill sang at the service, and we marched in and sat with the family.

Now Gary has made a complete about-face. Robin has said she wakes up in the night and finds Gary on his knees, praying out loud for forgiveness of all the bad things he's done to his mother. He protects me as an old sitting hen would protect her eggs. It was his idea that they stay over for the weekends so somebody would be here with me. Gary is even going to make dinner.

He has cirrhosis of the liver, and, thank the Lord, he can't take a drink any more. Now he goes to church and he prays at home, too. His wife Robin says, "How that man can quote Scripture. You all really brought him up right." He guides her. He's happier now than he's ever been in his adult life. Until a few months ago, he didn't have any place to stay or place to go. He couldn't work, so he went back to Robin and married her. They get along, even though he's weak and on medication. I am very, very happy that I've lived long enough to see this situation turn around.

Now Gary treats me like a baby. He won't let me spend a dime when he's around. He does all the washing and all the cooking, and he takes care of Robin's children as if they were his. Now he goes to church with me on Sunday, holds my hand, prays, and cries. You wonder where the young African American woman is going to find a good husband —like my son who does the washing, cooking, taking care of the house and the children. I would say he's been an ideal husband to Robin. But where would you find more Garys?

I pay Mrs. Cora next door to bring over breakfast and see that I'm safe in bed at night. And I'm taking piano lessons. That darling Frances Gordon in DeLand said she'd teach me for free because it was such an inspiration to the children and their families to see someone as old as me willing to learn. But I can't impose on LeRosa any longer to take me all the way over there. Right now I'm taking lessons from Isabel and playing Schubert. It is very difficult and hard for me to remember.

This has been a tough year—in the hospital four different times, four heart attacks and a new pace maker. Bill keeps trying to get my attention from heaven by sending me these dizzy spells and lack of oxygen to my heart. I have to shout at him: "No! I'm not ready yet."

There's something I still want to do: I want to write history books. I want to write about Seminoles and other Native Americans and other groups of African Americans, wherever they might be. I particularly want to write about the Africans in Tanzania.

I haven't used a computer yet, but Bettye Parham, the academic coordinator at DBCC, says she'll teach me. She said she'd do anything free for me. My cousin Doll or Jack or LeRosa will take me where I want to go. LeRosa wants me to come and live with her right now. She has a new large house with one bedroom marked Mae. But I don't want to do that. I need my privacy. And now that I've got new locks on the doors, I'm a little safer.

Back to the Future

This past January (1997) I retired from teaching, at least temporarily, to go on a lecture tour and write some books. However, *The Daytona Beach News-Journal* quoted me accurately: "I'm going to miss my teaching. I'm going to miss my students. I'm going to miss my co-workers. Teaching has been my life. So I'm like a displaced person."

First I had the NAACP Lifetime Service tribute in January, which involved declaring an "Annie Mae Walker Day" for Volusia County and some awards, including a lifetime distinguished service award. By February 1 I had my next teaching assignment—a full month of television and radio interviews and lecturing on Black history to schools and the library in Connecticut for Black History month. They scheduled me for four lectures a day. The entire trip was made in a wheelchair with my host wrapping my infected feet in bandages every night. I just had to tough it through. But the trip was a big success. Whew!

An article in the *Connecticut Post* described that part of that visit:

> There have been so many changes since I started teaching back then," [Walker] said. "Nowadays, children are less inhibited and seem happier. Their responses are so spontaneous. There is such a

freedom and happiness associated now with learning that wasn't there in the past....American history is Black history.

We are so excited about the information and songs she had shared with our students," second-grade teacher Joyce Pinkler said of Walker's visits. "She came to our class and taught the kids old spiritual songs."

She was so cool," said eight year-old Gary Aileen.

Walker has won the Martin Luther King Award, the Human Relations Award, the National Conference of Christian and Jews Award, and the National Sojourner Truth Award.

****

This *has* been a difficult year. I'm hooked up to oxygen still because my heart is beating too fast. My feet were infected for a whole year, so I haven't been able to walk, and I've been scared to death the doctor will amputate my feet. I take pain pills every four hours around the clock.

But just remembering the joy of being with those children! Yes, sir, that makes me feel so happy. The most enjoyment was at the home of my hostess, Michelle Rosa (the sister of my student, Angela, who accompanied me). She had four little girls. At first they all called me Dr. Walker, but I complained. I said I am a member of this family. The three year-old agreed and said everybody should call me "Mother." I agreed. (All my students and colleagues have called me Ma.)

The three year-old would knock on my door every morning to ask if I was sick. When I said no, she and her puppy would snuggle up in bed with me. It's the very first time I've been in an interracial family where the family on both sides are totally supported and so bonded.

I was so well received by them and the community that Bridgeport has invited me to come back next year. If God is willing and the pacemaker works, I'll go.

I need to spend some time at home now. There's still some history books I've intended to write all these years, especially the story of the Muslim groups in Tanzania and the history of the Seminoles and African-Americans' merger into our society. Bettye Parham, the beautiful academic coordinator at the college says she'll teach me to use a computer free. My cousins, Doll or Jack or LeRosa, will take me where I want to go.

I need my privacy. And now that I've got new locks on the doors, I'm a little safer. I discovered I can dial 911 in an emergency and just leave the phone off the hook. The police can get here without my even having to say a word.

I still take piano lessons every week, thanks to my grandson, Gary. He said, "Grandma, don't sit there and worry about Miss Raines moving. I have a wonderful music teacher, and I'm going to ask her to give you lessons, too. But Grandma, I'll tell you right now. She's tough."

"If Gary says I'm tough, then I'll have to take you," Frances Gordon said. And that's when we fell in love with each other, right then. I'm the only adult student she has, and now she's telling people I'm 84. I said, "Frances, get off it. Allow me to get 84. Until January 13, 1997, I'm only 83."

After 85 years I see big changes for Black people. The big change has come about with the young African-Americans. There's the excessive use of substances, mild-altering substances, and that hurts. That hurts very badly.

During the time when African-Americans were slaves, the masters could control their movement with fugitive slave laws and arrest them for vagrancy, but the one thing the master couldn't do was control their minds. And mind control is what's happening today. I don't know that it's hopeless. Efforts are being made to get crack out of the black neighborhood. These young Black people need to be shown that these guys that have the stuff distributed live on exotic islands with the big yachts and do not feel the effects of what's happening to the Black community.

One of the main reasons why my generation and the generation after me have lost some of the old traditional values is that we've been made ashamed of our heritage, our background. My father was one in a million. Every night before we children went to bed, he would tell us the history of slavery and what went on. Other Black families ignore it and try to pretend it never happened to their ancestors, do not want to face it. That's why so many Blacks have problems with identity issues.

Knowing both sides of my family in our history experienced violence and harsh treatment through no fault of their own, has resulted in a bitterness that is an admitted and fundamental part of my personality. However, it also means I don't believe in violence as a solution. I am committed to work endlessly in the liberating struggle for my people.

In so far as social mobility, there's been a great change—more interracial marriages, more integrated neighborhoods, and places like this college, where I could not reach years ago, but I can now teach and be recognized for my accomplishments.

What I know now is that the more integration and intermingling, the better the chances for good human relations to exist between Black and non-Black. I'm all for it. All for it. As I teach my students, there is no difference between people, just a difference in the color of the skin: Black skin simply has more melanin to protect it from harmful effects of the sun. Except for that speck of melanin, we're all alike.

Some well-meaning friends and relatives suggested I move to a retirement home. I was furious. That's for old folks, I told them. I don't want to move in with anybody. Don't you dare make a judgment of me as old!

You know, I've been fighting stereotypes of what I'm "supposed" to be as a Black woman all my life, and now I have to fight against ingrained dumb ideas about age limits. I still somehow have to teach people that nothing—absolutely nothing—is impossible once you set your heart on it.

Dr. Mae Walker's Legacy

The legacy of Dr. Annie Mae Walker shows how just one woman can change the lives of millions of others who struggle in a society that values wealth and prestige.

Black teachers now receive equal pay, a cause she fought for in Florida, even as her co-petitioner for equal pay had his home fire-bombed and lost his life. With the help of Eleanor Roosevelt, Mae escaped to New York and became the first black teacher in an all-white school—a job now common for African-American teachers.

The African-American studies program she created, even as she had her office fire-bombed and her life threatened, has now become common at colleges and universities throughout the United States.

At the time of her death on July 5, 1998, the Head Start model she pioneered at the request of President Lyndon B. Johnson in 1965, was still the one used throughout the United States. More than 25 million children have gone through what is considered one of the most successful government programs of all times. In 2015, CCR Analytics published the results by more than 11,500 California Head Start and Early Head Start parents. Ninety percent said that

Head Start helped them to get or keep a job, 92 percent said it helped them to enroll in an educational or training program, and 99 percent of families surveyed said Head Start helped them to improve their parenting skills. These results indicate that Head Start has a positive impact on the whole family, beyond the individual children who attend the program.

In 2009, David Deming discovered "those who attended Head Start showed stronger academic performance as shown on test scores for years afterward, were less likely to be diagnosed as learning-disabled, less likely to commit crime, more likely to graduate from high school and attend college, and less likely to suffer from poor health as an adult."

Those men Mae worked so closely with for civil rights, Dr. Martin Luther King, Jr., and Malcolm X, are regarded as national heroes. The same is true for her "foster mother" and mentor, Dr. Mary McLeod Bethune. And the progress made in anthropology and medicine, Mae once observed, is "destroying the myth of race. We've learned it just doesn't matter how much melanin we have in our skin. We are all related as God's children."

She had the most courage of anyone I have met in my life because she had everything against her. From that poor, motherless black child in a Florida turpentine camp emerged a woman who not only changed history, but, as one of her students proclaimed, "Dr. Walker's life is America's black history." She would enter the classroom with a walker and a smile on her face, ignoring terrible pain. "Hi, Mom," the students would greet her. Daytona Beach Community College added to the long list of her honors by giving her its Lifetime Achievement Award.

Her cousin, Lerosa Dixon, recalls that Mae "never complained and never gave in to her sickness." She proved all her doctors wrong by becoming the longest survivor of sarcoma and teaching and inspiring students until months before her death of a heart attack and then a stroke at age 85.

Dr. Walker remains a reminder of what values are most important. In spite of having suffered a heart attack and then a stroke hours before she passed, she was able to tell one of her caregivers a message she always remembered to tell everyone she met, "I love you."

Epilogue

Highlights of Dr. Mae Walker's Life

Born January 7, 1913, in Tomoka Land Turpentine Camp in what is now the Volusia Mall, sixth of 10 children, to Seminole mother and South Carolina-born Negro father.

Mother dies July 16, 1916, at age 27 years, 3 months and 12 days, giving birth to her ninth and tenth children, stillborn twins; Mae is 3 and a half.

Father takes Susie and Mae to Coom-Choo-Chee reservation; Minnie goes to Aunt Minnie; others farmed out with other relatives. He later brings them back to Daytona so Mae can become one of the five girls in Mrs. Bethune's Industrial School for Girls.

First stepmother, Mrs. Lilla, tries to decapitate Mae with an ax. Father sends wife & her two daughters away instantly.

Second stepmother, Missy, "Mrs. Ill Treatment," beats children; is alcoholic, prostitute; steals Mae's sewing machine.

Papa brings them back to Daytona so Mae can become one of Mrs. Bethune's girls in kindergarten. In third grade Mae organizes a night school to teach basic literacy to construction workers at night; charge is 50 cents a week. She teaches her own father to read and to write and assigns him a project to make a complete house out of match boxes. Later he builds the 10-room real house for his family.

In third grade she becomes boarding school student at Bethune-Cookman Industrial School for Girls in Daytona Beach.

1929: Runs away from home at age 13; forced to quit school in 9th grade; escape to West Palm Beach, where she cooks for Judge Chillingworth (before his wife and daughter were kidnapped and murdered).

Marries Odell Lambert at 15; he is physically and verbally abusive. Menial labor: cook for a family; laundry, pressing for cleaners; domestic work, 1930: Infant son William dies of meningitis at age 10 months.

Teaches at rural school in Bunnell; recruits students from potato field workers.

Divorces Odell Lambert.

1934: Returns to high school; does two years' work in one and becomes valedictorian. Meets Wendell Tooks. Mae also best friends with novelist/ storyteller/anthropologist Zora Neale Hurston.

August 23, 1935. **Marries Wendell Tooks.**

1937-38: Mae operates her own beauty shop in Miami. Sister Susie killed in accident. Mae adopts Dora's children: Lorenzo and Billy

First Lady Eleanor Roosevelt becomes her mentor; Mae does research to give her before Dumbarton Oaks Conference (the prelude to the UN). Two become friends.

. 1943 Mae goes back to college. A straight A student at Bethune-Cookman College, Mae graduates summa cum laude, first in her class on May 22, 1944.

As a teacher in Volusia County, she and a fellow Black teacher sue the State Dept. of Ed. for equal pay for Black teachers. Male teacher and his wife and family killed when KKK set fire bombs to the house.

Mae gets full graduate fellowship, becomes first Black student at the Bank Street College. Summers at Columbia University in New York. 1946: First Black woman to obtain M.A. in Education. Eleanor Roosevelt often greets Mae's students in park.

1946: Teacher at Brooklyn Community School. Works there for four years.

1954 She adopts abandoned bi-racial baby, Gary.

She founds the Freedom School '63, the first all-volunteer after-school school for students who failed the year before. After three years where no student failed the next year's schooling, State of New York took over the program.

June, 1965: Mae asked to create and direct one of the nation's first Head Start Program. It was such a success that her program model was mandated for State of NY.

1965: Mae becomes first Black woman to get M.A. in Sociology at Adelphi University, where she has attended the Jefferson School.

1965 Creates First Head Start Pre-School program in USA.

1967: Marries William Walker, chauffeur for Ella Fitzgerald. Divorces previous two husbands at the same time. He gets M.S.W. from SUNY.

1968: Hired as first professor of Black studies at State U of NY-Stony Brook; gets Ph.D. in Social/ Cultural Anthropology. Dissertation on Black studies programs in U.S. Specialty in American and Seminole Native American Cultures and History.

Activities with NAACP for Black studies result in her office door set on fire; her home in White neighborhood vandalized; she escapes to neighbor's house.

KKK burns cross on their front lawn.

Malcom X lives in their home until mosque built.

She joins Freedom Train with Dr. Martin Luther King. Goes to Birmingham. People throw rotten tomatoes and call her "Jerimiah" and "Nigger."

1970: Becomes first Black woman Danforth Scholar at Yale University. Has to wait a year for housing. Maya Angelou is a brief roommate.

AME Delegate to Liberia, West Africa for International Congress Meeting. 1970

Exchange Professor in Western Africa: Ghana (1972) Tanzania, (1973) and Nigeria (1974). Stands between Shirley Temple Black and Prime Minister of Nigeria to welcome Olympic athletes.

(1974)Initiated into Yoruba tribe in Nigeria; is given royal rank of Oshu, a title which also recognizes beauty and kindness.

1974: Returns to SUNY; Consultant to the State Department of Education, NY.

.In 1977: diagnosed with osteosarcoma, cancer of the spine. On Dec. 17, she is told to prepare to die, that she has a maximum life expectancy of less than six months.

1977: Retires; Moves back to Florida with Bill. Gary marries and has a son, Gary, Jr.

1979 Mae and Bill join faculty of Bethune-Cookman College. Teaches two years, then resigns because of problems with stairs and assignment to second floor classrooms.

1988: Becomes adjunct instructor of Social Studies and anthropology at Daytona Beach Community College.

1987 Honorary Doctor of Philosophy degree from Bank Street College.

1987: Goes to New York's Sloan-Kettering Cancer Hospital for a check-up in 1989. They bring out entire staff to celebrate "this living miracle," the only known person to survive this kind of cancer for so many years.

Mae speaks 8 languages: English, Latin, French, Spanish, Kiswahili, Yoruba, Ewe, Ashanti.

1992: Starts piano lessons; in 1996, still continuing weekly lessons and recitals with children who also take from Frances Gordon of DeLand.

Helps create museum for Black studies at Stetson University in DeLand.

1994: Recognized for Outstanding Lifetime Achievement by DBCC.

Husband Bill dies December 26, 1995.

Fall 1996 Mae plans to teach three classes at DBCC, business as usual.

January 1997 Mae retires again. Is honored by the NAACP for lifetime achievement.

Spring 1997 Mae goes on media and speechmaking tour in Connecticut

Famous Friends

Mary McLeod Bethune—was second mother to young Mae

Eleanor Roosevelt -- through Bethune-Cookman College

Ray Charles--her brother's best friend; lived in their home for a while.

Malcolm X lived in Mae's home for a while

Mrs. Alexander Graham Bell—wanted Mae to work for her

Arthur and Mary Miller & Marilyn Monroe—teacher of Miller's two children

Martin Luther King--walked on all his Peace Marches

Maya Angelou--brief roommate at Yale University

Ella Fitzgerald—Mae's husband was Ella's chauffeur

Shirley Temple Black --Olympic ceremonies in West Africa

Prime Minister of Nigeria

Mr. Rhodes -- of fellowship

Alice Walker

Paule Marshall, Black writer from West Indies

Adam Clayton Powell — minister at her church

Zora Neale Hurston — mentor in high school

Toni Morrison — colleague at State U of New York

Alice Walker — son Gary's teacher and husband of Mae's friend Scooby Doo

Notes from Mae Walker's VITAE

Dr. Walker has committed her life to the enlightenment of people, young and old, and of virtually every racial, religious, and ethnic group of the world. This is so because she has traveled, lectured, and taught in several states in the United States, in the Caribbean Countries, in Europe, and in Africa. That her commitment to promoting a spirit of love, brotherhood and sisterhood among and between people is real and profound is evidenced not merely by the number of years she has studied and taught in the areas of academics and human relations, but by the voluntary service she has rendered in predominantly Black communities. It was in this capacity that Dr. Walker came to merit and receive several awards for outstanding services:

1. The "Sojourner Truth Award" from the Black Business and Professional Women, Suffolk County, NY. 1955.

2. Outstanding Educator Award from Suffolk County, NY NAACP for the founding and directing a "Freedom School" for underachieving Black students, 1963.

3. The Martin Luther King award for work in the area of Human Relations from the Suffolk County New York Human Relations Commission, 1965.

4. The "Outstanding Leadership Award" from the Leadership Training for Black Youth Organization for volunteer-teaching Black History to school drop-out youth, 1966.

5. Outstanding Leadership Award from the National Conference of Christians and Jews for promoting the cause of goodwill and understanding among the people of our nation. 1969

6.　Outstanding Teacher of the Year Award from the Women Senate, Bethune-Cookman College, 1978.

7.　Outstanding Services toward Humanity Award from BCC Faculty and Students, Award, Department of Social Sciences. 1979

8.　Certificate of Recognition as Outstanding Instructor at the DBCC. 1988

9. Lifetime Achievement Award from DBCC 1995.

10. NAACP Lifetime Achievement Award, Jan. 1997.

Annotated Bibliography

"Annie Mae Walker Named Equal Opportunity Chairman Professor." Photo captain.

Stony Brook News-Bulletin .16 October 1974.

Beier, Ulli. *The Return of the Gods: The Sacred Art of Susanne Wenger.* New York: Cambridge UP, 1975. Examines how European artist Susanne Wenger has been able to preserve the sacred grove to the goddess Oshun in Nigeria, how she has helped liberate women through the Yoruba religion.

Bethune-Cookman College Bulletin: 1978-80. Daytona Beach, FL, 1978. Gives history of the College and schedule of classes and events during the years that Bill and Annie Mae Walker served on the faculty, she for the second tenure.

Black Students United. "Warning." *Statesman* [Stony Brook, NY] 18 March 1970: 1.Serves notice that "the next incident perpetrated against Black people, whether small or large, will be taken as an act of open aggression against the Black community at large," and that students will retaliate in self-defense.

Bullard, Sara (ed). *Free At Last: A History of the Civil Rights Movement and Those Who Died in the Struggle."* Montgomery, Ala.: Southern Poverty Law Center, 30.

Callendar, Robert. "Blacks To Transcend Martyrdom." *Statesman* [Stony Brook, NY] 18 March 1970: 1. Declares that "White racists have declared open season on Black people," and that "will create one of the most classic examples of evolution which will cause Darwin to turn over in his grave."

Clark, James C. "Late 19th Century Slaves." *Florida Magazzine* 19 May 1991: 15. Presents historical view of turpentine camp owners in Florida from 1981 to 1944. Notes attempts by President Theodore Roosevelt and Mary Grace Quackenbos, a New York reformer, against "the existence of virtual slavery in Southern Florida."

Clarke, John Henrik. *Malcolm X: The Man and His Times.* NY: Collier, 1969. Hardcover edition by

---

Macmillan. Considers the meaning and influence of Malcolm X through views of Civil Rights leaders, and presents dialogues with and speeches by the founder of the Black Panthers.

Dees, Jesse Walter. *The College Build on Prayer: Mary McLeod Bethune.* NY: Ganis & Harris, 1953. Examines the life of the founder of Bethune- Cookman College in Daytona Beach. Provides a spiritual, inspirational approach to the story of the beginnings of the college as Daytona Normal and industrial Institute for Girls in 1904 "with $1.50 and five little girls" to her listing as one of the 10 most important women in the world.

Drewal, Margaret Thompson. *Yoruba Ritual: Performers, Play, Agency.* Bloomington: Ind. UP, 1992. Explains theory and method in the study of ritual performance, the theory of self in Yoruba religion, and looks at how performances are shaped, especially in terms of gender.

Eber, Stu. "Recognize Prejudices." *Statesman* [Stony Brook, NY] 18 March 1970: 1. Presents opinion that Blacks on campus "have reached the point where they feel any attacks on Blacks should be met in kind," and lists other incidents which feed "seeds of hate and destruction." Urges students to "deal with others as people, not political or social labels."

Glassman, Steve, and Kathryn Lee Seidel. *Zora in Florida.* Orlando: Central FLA UP, Contains a series of essays by writers concerned with Zora Neale Hurston's life and literature relating to Florida, including the period when she taught at Bethune-Cookman College in 1933-34 and was a friend of Mae Walker.

Gleason, Judith. *Orisha: The Gods of Yorubaland.* NY: Athenium, 1971. Tells the story of Yoruba religious figures from viewpoint of anthropologist who was initiated into religion in a ceremony with Mae Walker in Nigeria.

Goldfield, David R. *Black, White, and Southern: Race Relations and Southern Culture,1940 to the Present* Baton Rouge: LA State UP, 1990. Looks at the "regional trauma of immense proportions, paid for in blood and souls and minds" in terms of "redemption that southerners are wrestling"(xv). Deals with issues of White supremacy, civil rights, and current race relations.

Harley, Sharon, and Rosalyn Terborg-Penn. *The Afro-American Woman: Struggles and Images.* __ Port Washington, NY: Kennikat, 1978. Positions historical perspectives of Black women through the 19th and 20th centuries with images of Black women in Afro-American poetry, and includes a special focus on three activists: Anna

L. Cooper, Nannie Burroughs, and the 1952 Vice-Presidential campaign of Charlotta A. Bass.

Harnack, Roger. "South Campus 'Living Legend' is Honored." *Observer* [New Smyrna Beach, FL] 18 Feb. 1995: A1,5. Reports on celebration to honor Dr. Walker for "commitment to education and multiculturalism."

Hartman, Ronnie. "Unknown Vandals Deface Black Studies Office Door." *Statesman* [Stony Brook, NY] 18 March 1970: 1. Describes burning of Dr. Mae Walker's office door and a "scrawled death note, saying 'It's on you.'"

Hill, Ruth Edmonds, ed. "Introduction" *The Black Women: Oral History Project* 1-10.Westport, Conn.: Meckler 1991, i-xx. Discusses how oral history "deliberately creates primary source material for use by future historians." Notes the events which precipitated great change for Blacks, including emancipation from slavery, establishment of Bethune-Cookman College, and 20th century civil rights events.

Hine, Darlene Clark; Wilma King, and Linda Reed, eds.

"We Specialize in the WhollyImpossible": A Reader in Black Women's History. Brooklyn, NY: Carlson, 1995. Incorporates political and social theories of African-American culture with those of African, Caribbean, and Canadian women from the 18th through the 20th centuries. Contains 32 essays by scholars on issues relevant to Black women.

Hughes, Langston. "Mother to Son". *The Poetry of the Negro 1746-1949*. Garden City, NY: Doubleday, 1949. The Country Life Press, 1st edition, 119. Presents an anthology of poems of well-known Black poets and historical themes.

Lerner, Gerda. "A College on a Garbage Dump: Mary McLeod Bethune." In *Black Women in White America*. NY: Pantheon, 1972, 134-142. Give biographical and historical data on Bethune- Cookman College in Daytona Beach, told in autobiographical sketch.

McBride, Shannon. "Educator Saluted as 'Living History.'" *News-Journal* [Daytona Beach, FL) Daily Journal section. 18 Feb. 1995:1-2. Focuses on evening of tributes to Mae Walker during a salute at Daytona Beach Community College.

Morgan, Jean. "Illness No Obstacle for 78 Year-Old DBCC Instructor." *News-Journal* 12 Feb., 1991 [Daytona Beach, FL]: C1. Discusses how Dr. Mae Walker continues to teach anthropology and social studies in spite of a degenerative bone disease and constant pain. Quotes Walker: "It's a selfish reason. I feel I learn from my students every day. It's reciprocal. I give to them, they give to me."

"Mrs. Mae Walker To Teach at Stony Brook U." *Long Island Weekly Voice*. 7 July 1966.Interviews the new professor at the State University of New York, discussing sentimental farewell ceremonies at Plainview elementary schools, remarking that "people are always drawn to her" and announces Walker's appointment as the first and only woman on the Human Relations Commission of Suffolk County.

"NCNG Holds Food Festival in Bay Shore." *Long Island Weekly Voice: Clubwoman*, 5 April 1965, 1. Promotes activities of the National Council of Negro Women, a national organization founded by Dr. Mary McLeod Bethune, especially Head Start, directed by Annie Mae Walker in Long Island. Photo included.

"1973 Honoree: Dr. Annie Mae McClary Walker." *Leadership Training Institute* (printed program) April 1973, np. Photo included. Recognizes achievements of Walker leading to her named recipient of 1973 Leadership Award. Cites the work of "Mom," which is of "special significance to the familiarity in the relationship for Black people, which is a concept of family-hood and the love and respect engendered through kinship that unifies Blacks as a people, as a nation." Says Blacks have a "special responsibility of extending themselves as Common Mother and Father."

"Noted Anthropologist Joins South Campus Faculty." *Observer* [New Smyrna Beach, FL] 2 August 1991: B1. Incorporates biographical information on Dr. Mae Walker with information on how to sign up for her classes."

Oduyoy, Modupe. *Yoruba Names: Their Structure and Their Meanings*. Ibadan, Nigeria: Daystar P: 1972. Gives a minimum grammar of the Yoruba language to serve as language learning aid; notes most Yoruba names are structured like phrases and sentences, and most have extant meanings.

Pond, T.A. "Statement." *Statesman* [Stony Brook, NY] 18 March, 1970: 1. Presents viewpoint of the President of the State University of New York with public apology to Dr. Mae Walker and others.

"Professor Walker Awarded Danforth Fellowship in Black Studies." "Stony Brook News Briefs," Office of University Relations, State U of New York at Stony Brook: 23 March 1970. Announces the $7,500 award which Walker plans to use at Yale University and includes a congratulatory statement from SUNY President T.A. Pond.

Reiners, Arnold C. "Trustee's Position." *Amityville Record* [Long Island] 30 April 1964:2. Defends Board of Education's positions and claims charges regarding de facto segregation are spurious.

Rogers-Rose, La Frances, ed. *The Black Woman*. Beverly Hills: Sage, 1980. Looks at social demographic characteristics of Black women in historical context from 1940 to 1975 and deals with the self/group actualization of Black women in America. Charges that Blacks have been historically undercounted and the stability of the Black family misconstrued in negative ways.

Smith, Elaine M. "Mary McCleod Bethune and the National Youth Administration." In *Clio Was a Woman: Studies in the History of American Women*, Mabel E. Deutrich and Virginia C. Purdy, eds. Washington, D.C.: Howard UP, 1980, 149 - 177. Focuses on life of the founder of Bethune-Cookman College during the period when she directed the National Youth Administration for the Roosevelt administration, dealing especially with issues of Negro leadership in all avenues of American Life.

Smith, John P. "Cultural Preservation of the Sea Island Gullah: A Black Social Movement in the Post-Civil Rights Era." *Rural Sociology* 56(2), 1991, 284-298. Examines Gullah culture from historical perspective, beginning with transfer of slaves from Africa, focusing on how isolation factors preserved African culture and a unique language which is similar to a cajun English. Looks at how this land base for the Black culture there was changed by land developers in the late 1970's.

Thompson, Robert. "Congresswoman Allies Herself With Youth." *Statesman.* [Stony Brook, NY] 18 March, 1970: 5. Presents views of Shirley Chisholm that "the time has come when Blacks can no longer put band aids over sores" and calls for Black men and women to "fight the battle"against oppression.

Tindall, George Brown. *South Carolina Negroes: 1877-1900.* Kingsport, TENN: Kingsport, 1966. Traces "the post- Reconstruction developments in Negro life and institutions and in race relations that are pregnant with meaning for the present day" (vii) in terms of recovery from slavery, decline of Republicanism, migration, the Negro Church and education (at the time James McClary lived in the State).

Wade-Lewis, Margaret. "Lorenzo Down Turner: Pioneer African- American Linguist."*The Black Scholar* 21 (4), 10-21. Examines Turner's work in Gullah, the Creole-English spoken exclusively by African-Americans along the coast of Georgia and South Carolina, and in the Sea Islands, and used in literature such as Joel Chandler Harris's Uncle Remus: His Songs and His Sayings. Notes features of Gullah include absence of final consonants and absence of *theta* and *eth.*

Walker, Annie Mae McClary. *Black Churches in America.* American Broadcasting Co.. 7 November 1976. Discusses the pre-Civil War and post-Civil war history of churches in terms of political as well as spiritual significance in hour-long special program written by and featuring Dr. Walker.

_____ *De Facto Segregation for Amityville Children.* Darrynane, New York: Free, 1964. Charges that a neighborhood school with primarily Black students handicaps its students for life through "poor preparation and insufficient challenges" from the first grade forward in a system that "cheats all children, both Negro and White."

_____ "For a School Board That Will Lead Amityville to Better Education." *Amityville Record* [Long Island] 30 April 1964:2. Endorses Mae Walker's platform for the Suffolk County School Board,"including charges of "de facto segregation" by the current Board of Education.

_____ *A History of Education of Afro-Americans in America.* Milburn, N.J.: RF, 1975. Examines 100 years of history of Black Americans from their education in ante bellum America and the CivilWar to problems in education through the 1960s and includes comments on racial differences on Black intelligence tests, issues with Negro colleges, and strategies for humanizing testing of minorities. Also includes essays by prominent Black educators including Robert M. Hutchins,Roosevelt Johnson, Lawrence Crouchett, Janette Hoston Harris, and others.

_____ *The Implementation and Development of Interdisciplinary Programs in Black Studies in the University.* NY: East Coast University, 1970. Doctoral Dissertation examines how Black Studies programs emerged and suggests a broad range of curriculum to be implemented in the academy.

____ *Portrait of the John and Sarah Jane Nunn Family: Roots-Ghana, West Africa.* Daytona Beach, FL: Wesley Bros., 1983.

"Walker, Annie Mae." *Who's Who Among Black Americans,* V I- XII, 1975/76-1997/98.

Gives biographical information listing education, special expertise in anthropology, and numerous awards received by Walker during her lifetime.

Zigler, Edward and Jeanette Valentine. *Project Head Start: A Legacy of the War on Poverty.* New York: Free Press, 1979. Presents more than 20 research-based articles by educators as well as historical information which charts the beginning of Head Start programs in the United States, beginning in 1965.

INDEX

232

Reflect and Respond

Chapter 1: Death of a Childhood

♣   In recounting her early life at the turpentine camp, Mae looks at the primitive, unsanitary conditions and poverty. How is this similar or different from the conditions facing current migrant workers in Florida and the United States?

♣   How does the peculiar dialect of the rural Blacks isolate and cause discrimination?

♣   This chapter discusses the hierarchical difference between skin shades of African-Americans? Why or why not would you believe this is important today?

♣   What points does Mae make about how Blacks could learn basic literacy in those times?

♣   Mae was considered "evil" because she was a constant bed-wetter. Do you think people with this problem are still shamed by others?

♣   **Respond:** Examine how and why this pre-school age child was able to overcome obstacles of physical and emotional abuse, loss of her mother and siblings, responsibility of care for a baby sister, and extreme poverty.

Chapter 2: Life with 'Mrs. Ill Treatment'

♣   Expectations both at Mrs. Bethune's Training School for Negro Girls and at home were that female children spend hours a day learning domestic chores, including sewing, gardening, and cleaning. How does this differ from "training" children today receive? Is it still different for girls than for boys?

♣   Mae talks about name-calling: a savage, Crackers, Niggers, "Playing the Dozens." Consider how labels still affect the self-esteem of an ethnic group and/or a child.

♣   Even as a small child, Mae found a way to educate workers at the turpentine camp who lacked basic literacy. In what ways can a child today help educate others around her/him?

Chapter 3: Mama Mame and the Big Shots

♣   Mrs. Bethune insisted her girls show patriotism. Is this a quality still encouraged in schools today? Why or why not?

♣   Mae says Langston Hughes's poem, "Life Ain't No Crystal Stair" inspired her life. Is there a poem or story that acts as a mantra for your own life? What is the important underlying message for you?

♣   Being made to wear cheap, ugly shoes felt so traumatic that Mae ran away from home and destroyed her feelings of well-being. How important are clothes to your self-image?

♣   Respond: In Daytona Beach, whites lived by the beach; Blacks lived west of the train tracks. Are the invisible lines of socio-economic or ethnic groups still drawn today?

Chapter 4: A Thirteen Year-Old 'Grown Up'

♣   Out of school, Mae took French and Latin lessons at night from an Episcopal priest. What can a drop-out do today to get an education?

♣   Mae found herself the victim of her employer's sexual abuse and then her husband's physical abuse, but believed the only escape was running away again. What are other options for victims today?

♣   Respond: Mae found herself having to aid and abet her employers' illegal business. In which ways are some people today still in danger of being victimized?

Chapter 5: "The 'Sheik' and Zora Neale Hurston

♣   Ashamed that her step-mother was an alcoholic, Mae begged her not to drink when she brought her boyfriend home to meet the family, but Missy got drunk anyway. What do you think a family member can do to deal with a situation like that?

♣   Bethune-Cookman offered jobs to help students get through school. Is this feasible for schools today to help financially-strapped students with the menial jobs they offered?

Chapter 6: Licking the Pots in Sorrow's Kitchen

♣   Unwanted sexual overtures and demeaning behaviors from white employers put Mae and her husband, Wendell, as well as the chauffer, Walter, in jeopardy. How can employees deal with this kind of behavior so they don't have to run away?

♣   Mae is advised to lie about being offered more money so that the Montgomerys would double her salary. If what she calls "exaggerating" were the only way to earn enough to live on, could you consider any other choice? Why or why not?

♣   Respond: What qualities within herself did it take for Mae to deal with heart ache, starting a business by gambling, becoming ill, and deciding to go back to school? Is going back to school the best choice when facing obstacles?

Chapter 7: My Mentor—Eleanor Roosevelt

♣   How does Mae's description of the first lady match those qualities you learned about Eleanor Roosevelt in school?

♣   Why do you think the wife of a U.S. President would come to an African-American school and become involved with students?

♣   Respond: What program at your school would you like for the First Lady to come help with? What kind of role would you play?

Chapter 8: The Black Scam for Teachers

♣   Mae joins two activist organizations to try to effect equality for Blacks, the NAACP and the Black Teachers Association. What organization would you join to make a change that you care about—for students, athletes, persons with disabilities, the homeless, etc.?

♣   As a married woman, Mae is not allowed to make changes in her life without approval of her husband or their family. How would that be different today and why?

♣   Consider what factors and approval are needed for you to change direction in a career, residence, or relationship.

Chapter 9: Bombs and Bank Street

♣   Mae recognizes that her lack of money and color of her skin make her a social outcast? Do we ostracize others today based on skin color, cultural differences or howmuch money one has?

♣   As a teacher, the most important part with students is to "take their ideas and put them first and guide them and direct them along lines they wish to take." Do you recall teachers who did that with you—or with your children or sibilings?

♣   Mae's two heritages, the Seminoles and Blacks, had opposing views of man's relationship to the earth. The first wanted to preserve the environment while the latter wanted to change environment to further society. To which do you subscribe?

Chapter 10: Marilyn Monroe and the Shrink

♣   This anecdote about Marilyn Monroe as a doting mother, a chatty, outgoing cook-at-home wife—or one accused of giving a child beer!—conflicts with our traditional images of the famous actress. Was she just "acting" the homebody?

♣   When Mae can finally understand why her childhood relationship with her alcoholic stepmother was bad, she feels so good she goes shopping for new draperies and buys her first Christmas tree. Do you think "retail therapy" really works?

♣   Mae's purchase of her dream home causes the white neighborhood to collapse and her husband to go back to Florida "where people have sense." Does moving to a new place change your feelings of your own identity? Are people different inside because they live in one part of the country rather than another?

Chapter 11: Bill Walker and Ella Fitzgerald

♣   Mae lays down the gauntlet and tells Bill it's "sobriety through A.A. or divorce." Do you believe one person can really be effective in getting another to quit drinking and get help?

♣   She advises Ella Fitzgerald to quit eating cake because "You're fat enough already." Is that helpful advice or would it feel like terrible judgmental behavior?

♣   With Bill, it is "kind of like, I'll make me a man." She plans to change a street person into a professional social worker. Can we really change who another person is?

Chapter 12: Marching with the King

♣   Mae puts her career, her marriage, her son, and her life at risk by becoming an activist marching with Dr. Martin Luther King. What would it take for you to go through that kind of risk for a cause?

♣   Through Dr. King, leaders are taught passive resistance. What do ethnic groups do now to protest what they see as discrimination?

♣   Mae arranges for students to secretly come to her house to take an exam so they have a chance to graduate. What would the outcome be for a teacher planning to do that today?

Chapter 13: Freedom School and a Run for the Board

♣   By creating an after-school mentoring program, not one at-risk child failed. What would it take today to get this kind of project going in your local schools?

♣   Some believe *de facto* segregation still exists as we mandate that children go to school in their home neighborhoods. Is it important to eliminate this? What are the prospects for students in schools that receive the State grade of D or F?

Chapter 14: Malcolm X and Head Start

♣   Malcolm X was one of the most radical and controversial black Muslim leaders of his day. Why would Mae take him to live at her home when his anti-white messages went against her own beliefs? What were the consequences for her?

♣   President Lyndon Johnson called Mae and asked her to create a model for his new Head Start program. What kind of program do you believe young children need to become successful in life?

♣   Why do you think Head Start became so widespread and successful?

Chapter 15: The University Fights Back

♣   Mae becomes the first director of a Black Studies program—with no staff and no phone in a windowless office and no money. What kinds of things did or could she do to make this successful?

♣   Mae's office is fire bombed and the words "It's on you" scrawled in chalk on the door. What would you do if you felt you were targeted and in danger because of taking a stand?

♣   The university in fact banishes Mae off campus for a semester under the "honor" of making her a Danforth Scholar at Yale. Do you think businesses and universities play politics like that today with supposed awards and paid vacations?

Chapter 16: Maya Angelou and the 'Great Queen'

♣ Yale offered no housing for Blacks, so Mae was forced to stay in an off-campus apartment with a roommate chosen by the university. What kinds of messages did this send to her about the honor of being a Danforth Scholar?

♣ Maya Angelou's well-known personal history is as traumatic as Mae's. What else do these two women have in common? This was long before Maya wrote a self-poem about being a "Phenomenal Woman."

♣ Mae, like Zora Neale Hurston, becomes a member of divinity of an African voo doo religion, Yoruba, which "gives children, cures disease and is capable of fulfilling all wishes." Why would someone give up their lifelong protestant religion to enter a mystical one?

♣ Blackness "is the source from whence comes Love/ From whence comes Passion/From when comes Beauty/From whence comes Creativity/And all Spiritual vibrations/For the Planet Earth." Does this statement from Mae's poem coincide or contradict your own beliefs? Is so, how?

Chapter 17: Off to Africa and Beyond

♣ As the university next sends Mae to Ghana, she has learned to speak 10 languages. How could learning a new language change your perspective on other nations or races?

♣ A friend of the Pulitzer Prize winner, Chinua Achebe, Mae asks: "It is possible for a man to gain knowledge of who he is, that is his identity, his sense of greatness or weakness, through independent thought...or must he depend on collective thoughts and opinions of his clansmen or a determination of his actions through which his true identity is revealed?" How would you answer that question?

Chapter 18: A New Book: A Terminal Diagnosis

♣ When Mae is told she has just six months to live, she decides to come back to Florida and make a goal to learn how to play "Moonlight Sonata" on the piano. With that diagnosis, what would be a specific goal on your "bucket list"?

♣ Mae also joins the board of directors of a pre-school and decides to become a part-time college professor, illness notwithstanding. How important would it be for you to give to others what you could, even if you don't have much time left to do it?

Chapter 19: Home at Last

♣ Mae bemoans the loss of the Black church as the major influence of life. What is replacing that for both white and Black young people in America today?

♣ Mae wants to write history books so people today can understand the significance of problems in her day. What problems would you have her focus on in today's society?

Chapter 20: Back to the Future

♣ When Mae retires at age 85, she says she feels like a "displaced person." How does your job determine your own feelings about identity and usefulness as a citizen?

♣ In spite of her disability, Mae wants privacy and the feeling of being in her own home. How do we prevent that from happening for most aging people who are unable to get around on their own?

♣ Mae teaches her students, "There is no difference between people, just a difference in the color of the skin." Why or why not do you believe this is true?

Chapter 21: Dr. Mae Walker's Legacy

♣ Mae can point to changes she made for all Black people and for all children who attended Head Start. What are the hallmarks of your own legacy? What specifically would you like people to remember?